The Great Bible Challenge

The Great Bible Challenge

BOB PHILLIPS

HARVEST HOUSE PUBLISHERS
Eugene, Oregon 97402

Unless otherwise noted, all verses
are from the King James Version of the Bible.

THE GREAT BIBLE CHALLENGE
formerly *Heavenly Fun*

Copyright © 1990 by Harvest House Publishers
Eugene, Oregon 97402

ISBN 1-56507-216-2

Printed in the Unites States of America.

94 95 96 97 98 99 – 10 9 8 7 6 5 4 3 2 1

Introduction

I n our fast-paced society we often do not take time to have fun.
Sometimes we even feel guilty when we take a moment to relax.
When was the last time you slowed down and got your mind off the
pressures of a busy life? When was the last time you treated yourself to a
mini-vacation?

HEAVENLY FUN is designed to provide many hours of satisfying
entertainment, growth, and learning. It will give you bite-sized escapes to
refresh your mind and spirit. You'll get a big kick out of coming up with
solutions to the:

- Word Hunts
- Versigrams
- Tail Tags
- Patchword Puzzles
- Anagrams
- Bible Riddles
- Impossible Mazes
- and much more

You can sharpen your skills, test your Bible knowledge, and challenge
your mind all at the same time. You may like to use some of the puzzles
with your family as a mealtime diversion or as a method of learning while
traveling by car. Some of the games and riddles lend themselves to a
group challenge at a Bible study or Sunday school class. You may want to
share HEAVENLY FUN with a shut-in or someone who's in the hospital.
Try sending a copy to a missionary friend as a change of pace.

Some of the puzzles are easy and some are more difficult. It wouldn't be
fun if they were too easy. So just jump right into whatever catches
your fancy.

Have a great time. If you get stuck, the answers are in the back of the book. You can peek if you want to — no one will be watching.

We hope you won't struggle too much — just enough to experience the joy of learning and the satisfaction of solving a problem through your own resourcefulness. If you like these puzzles and have some of your own ingenious variations that you think others would enjoy, drop us a note and include them.*

— Bob Phillips
Hume, California

*Bible puzzles, riddles, and games — along with clean jokes — can be mailed to:

P.O. Box 9363
Fresno, CA 93792

Who Said It?

For each quote listed below, see if you can identify which of the following four people said it: Jeremiah, Agur, David, or Solomon.

1. "The Lord is my shepherd; I shall not want."

_____

2. "Cursed be the man that trusteth in man."

_____

3. "As far as the east is from the west..."

_____

4. "Peace, peace, when there is no peace..."

_____

5. "The way of transgressors is hard."

_____

6. "Of making many books there is no end."

_____

7. "A soft answer turneth away wrath."

_____

8. "Give me neither poverty nor riches."

_____

9. "A prudent wife is from the Lord."

_____

10. "Put a knife to thy throat."

_____

Quotation Puzzle

In the puzzle below, fit the letters of each column into the boxes directly above them. The letters may or may not go into the boxes in the same order in which they are listed. It is up to you to decide which letter goes into which box. Once a letter is used, cross it off the bottom half of the diagram and do not use it again. Some letters have been entered into boxes to help you get started, and those letters have been crossed off. Black squares are used to separate the words of the quotation. When the diagram is filled in, you will find the completed quotation by reading the boxes horizontally.

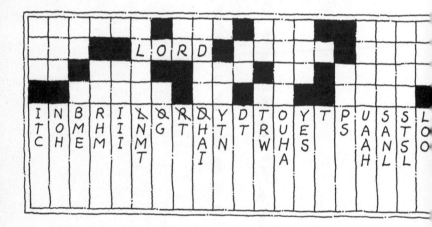

Help Lydia

Lydia, the seller of purple, needs to find her two longest ribbons. These ribbons start and end at the top of the tangled maze below. See if you can help her find them.

Occupation Match

See if you can match the names of Bible characters with their occupations.

1. Agur _____	A. Commander
2. Lazarus _____	B. Physician
3. Noah _____	C. Hunter
4. Cain _____	D. Carpenter
5. Cornelius _____	E. Tax collector
6. Joseph _____	F. Beggar
7. Benaiah _____	G. Author
8. Gamaliel _____	H. Boat builder
9. Matthew _____	I. Officer
10. Balaam _____	J. Centurion
11. Ishmael _____	K. Second in command
12. Nimrod _____	L. Doctor of law
13. Joshua _____	M. Founder of a race
14. Potiphar _____	N. False prophet
15. Luke _____	O. Builder of a city

Things That Happen
With Conversion

In the following word hunt see if you can find 27 things that happen with conversion. Begin with any letter and move one letter at a time to the right, left, up, down, or diagonally. When you find a word, draw a circle around it.

```
C  A  N  R  E  C  O  N  C  I  L  I  A  T  I  O  N
F  L  O  C  M  A  D  E  Z  I  C  H  L  O  V  E  P
O  V  A  M  O  L  W  A  S  H  I  N  G  S  J  B  R
R  R  T  D  E  L  I  V  E  R  E  D  K  A  S  L  E
G  G  O  O  D  E  S  H  E  I  R  M  R  N  A  V  S
I  P  S  I  N  D  T  O  P  E  R  F  E  C  T  I  E
V  R  J  O  Y  T  S  O  N  S  H  I  P  T  A  T  R
E  O  E  B  A  D  R  A  N  S  O  M  R  I  C  R  V
N  P  A  D  O  P  T  I  O  N  A  T  O  F  C  A  A
E  I  O  N  E  L  E  C  T  E  D  I  V  I  E  N  T
S  T  K  I  N  M  A  D  E  Z  I  T  I  C  P  S  I
S  I  M  E  R  C  P  K  I  N  D  N  D  A  T  L  O
E  A  D  N  F  A  I  T  H  E  S  S  E  T  E  A  N
M  T  H  A  P  P  I  W  I  S  D  Y  N  I  D  T  O
E  I  R  E  M  I  S  S  I  O  N  E  C  O  M  E  R
F  O  R  E  K  N  O  W  N  R  N  A  E  N  G  D  A
R  N  J  U  S  T  I  F  I  C  A  T  I  O  N  G  E
```

11

Jacob

Genesis 25:24–37:1

1. Isaac sent Jacob to the house of Bethuel who lived in _Padanaram_

2. Jacob had a dream of a ___ladder___ set on the earth with the top reaching to heaven.

3. Ascending and descending on the object in Jacob's dream were ___angels___.

4. Who was at the top of the object in Jacob's dream? _The Lord_

5. Jacob named the place where he had the dream ___Bethel___.

6. Jacob had an uncle who lived in Haran whose name was ___Laban___.

7. Jacob's uncle had two daughters named ___Rachel___ and ___Leah___.

8. Jacob fell in love with which of his uncle's daughters? ___Rachel___

9. Jacob worked ___7___ years to have the hand of ___Rachel___ in marriage.

10. ___Rachel___ stole some ___images___ from her father, ___Laban___.

11. Jacob served his father-in-law, ___Laban___, for ___14___ years for his two daughters and ___6___ years for the cattle he earned.

12. Jegarsahadutha and Galeed were actually ___a heap of stones___

A. Laban

B. Fourteen

C. Bethel

D. Leah

E. Angels

F. Seven

G. Padanaram

H. Ladder

I. Images

J. Six

K. The Lord

L. Rachel

M. A heap of stones

Bible Labyrinth

Hidden in the following Bible labyrinth is a verse from the Bible. Start at the top arrow and move one space at a time to the right, left, up, or down. You should finish the verse at the bottom arrow.

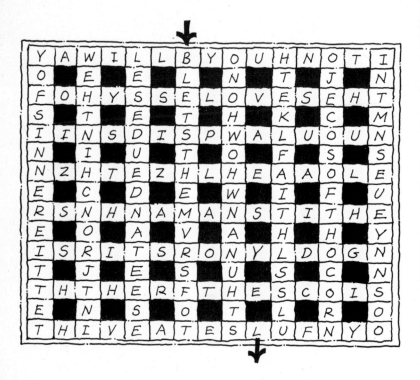

Name the Event

The picture below illustrates a Bible event, story, or verse. See if you can guess which Bible event, story, or verse the picture is illustrating.

_____

_____

_____

_____

_____

Where in the Bible is this event, story, or verse found?

_____

Versigram

Unscramble the following familiar Bible verses.

1. meCo otnu em, lal ey atht balruo nda ear aehyv dalne, nad I lwil

   Come unto me, all ye that labour and are heavy laden, and I will

   veig ouy stre.

   give you rest.

2. orF eht onS fo nam si meoc ot kese nda ot veas atht hcihw saw tsol.

   For the Son of man is come to seek and to save that which was lost.

3. reheT lashl otn yna nam eb blae to dnats refoeb hete lal the ysda

   There shall not any man be able to stand before thee all the days

   fo yth efil: sa I saw ithw osMse, os I liwl eb ithw ehte: I ilwl

   of thy life: as I was with Moses, so

   otn aifl ehte, onr orfksae ehte.

   will I be with thee. I will not fail thee nor forsake thee.

4. seJsu wsnreade and dias tnou ihm, "ilyVre, ilyvre, I yas ntou hete,

   Jesus answered and said unto him, Verily verily I say unto thee,

   cxtpee a nam be ronb agnia, eh natcon ese hte gndikmo fo oGd."

   except a man be born again, he cannot see the kingdom of god.

5. nAd dGo laeldc hte mrmaifnte avHnee. ndA hte nevnegi dna hte

   And God called the firmament heaven. And the evening and the

   rnomngi rewe the cnodes yad.

   morning were the second day.

Quotation Puzzle

In the puzzle below, fit the letters of each column into the boxes directly above them. The letters may or may not go into the boxes in the same order in which they are listed. It is up to you to decide which letter goes into which box. Once a letter is used, cross it off the bottom half of the diagram and do not use it again. Some letters have been entered into boxes to help you get started, and those letters have been crossed off. Black squares are used to separate the words of the quotation. When the diagram is filled in, you will find the completed quotation by reading the boxes horizontally.

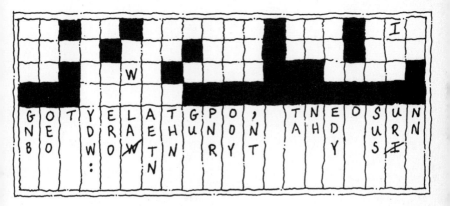

17

A Special Name

In seven moves, see if you can discover another name for Jesus.

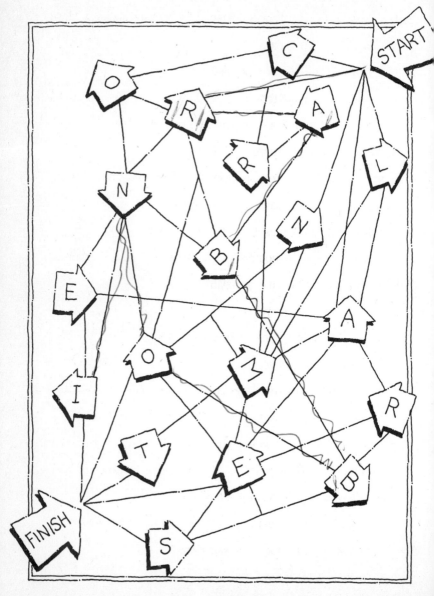

How Long?

1. How long was the infant Moses hidden to escape death?

   A. 1 month   B. 2 months   C. 3 months   D. 4 months

2. How long did the cloud cover the mount before God spoke to Moses?

   A. 3 days   B. 6 days   C. 9 days   D. 12 days

3. How long did the Feast of Tabernacles last?

   A. 7 days   B. 14 days   C. 1 month   D. 1 month and 7 days

4. How long were the spies searching the Promised Land?

   A. 30 days   B. 40 days   C. 60 days   D. 80 days

5. How long did a person remain unclean after touching a dead body?

   A. 3 days   B. 5 days   C. 7 days   D. 9 days

6. How long did marriage exempt a man from going to war?

   A. 1 month   B. 6 months   C. 1 year   D. It did not

7. How long did David reign over Judah?

   A. 3½ years   B. 7½ years   C. 8½ years   D. 12½ years

8. How long did it take Solomon to build the temple?

   A. 7 years   B. 12 years   C. 20 years   D. 30 years

9. How long did Job's three friends sit with him without speaking to him?

   A. 3 days   B. 7 days   C. 20 days   D. 1 month

10. How long were the Jews held captive in Babylon?

    A. 70 years   B. 90 years   C. 110 years   D. 130 years

11. How long were the Ninevites given to repent?

    A. 30 days   B. 40 days   C. 50 days   D. 60 days

12. How long did the first Egyptian plague last?

    A. 3 days   B. 5 days   C. 7 days   D. 9 days

Paul's Puzzle

Help Paul solve his puzzle by placing the 12 boxes, each containing two letters, into the empty diagram below. The puzzle will form four eight-lettered words reading across and down, as shown in the small puzzle to the left.

20

A Very Famous Place

Rearrange the letters and see if you can discover this very famous place.

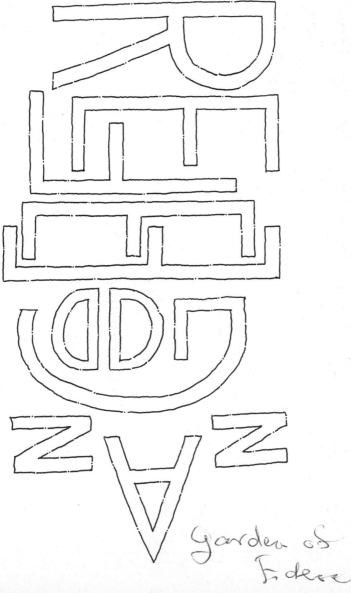

garden of
Eden

Isaac

Genesis 24:1–35:29

1. Abraham told his servant to select a wife for his son Isaac from among:

    A. The Canaanites

    B. His kindred

    C. The Hittites

    D. Those who lived in the land of Shur

2. Abraham's servant made an oath that he would get a bride for Isaac and sealed the oath by placing his hand where? _Under_ _Abraham's thigh_

3. The name of the bride selected for Isaac was:

    A. Rachel

    B. Ruth

    C. Remaliah

    D. Rebekah

4. What was the name of the father of Isaac's bride? _Bethuel_

5. Abraham married again after the death of Sarah and the name of his second wife was:

    A. Keturah

    B. Kedar

    C. Kishi

    D. Kushaiah

6. Abraham was 165 years of age when he died. ___True ✓ False /75

7. Isaac had two sons named _Jacob_ and _Esau_.

8. The sons of Isaac were twins and the first boy to be born was named ___Esau___.

9. The second twin born to Isaac was named ___Jacob___ and he was born holding on to his brother's:

   A. Hand

   B. Arm

   C. Heel

   D. Big toe

10. The firstborn son of Isaac had ___red___ colored hair.

11. Which of Isaac's sons sold his birthright? ___Esau___

12. The older son of Isaac stole the blessing of the younger son by
    younger
    cooking savory meat, putting on clothes belonging to the other brother, and covering his hands and neck with hair from the kid of a goat in order to deceive Isaac who could not see well at that time.

    ___True ✓ False

13. Isaac lived to be how old?

    A. 180

    B. 190

    C. 195

    D. 207

Name the Event

The picture below illustrates a Bible event, story, or verse. See if you can guess which Bible event, story, or verse the picture is illustrating.

_____

_____

_____

_____

Where in the Bible is this event, story, or verse found?

_____

Forgiveness – 70 x 7

Jesus told Peter that he should forgive others 70 x 7 times. Below, Peter has four opportunities to forgive, represented by four hexagons. There are six circles along the outside lines of each of the four hexagons. Can you place the proper numbers in the circles so that each hexagon totals 70? Each of the numbers can be used only once. Six numbers have been placed in the circles to give you a head start.

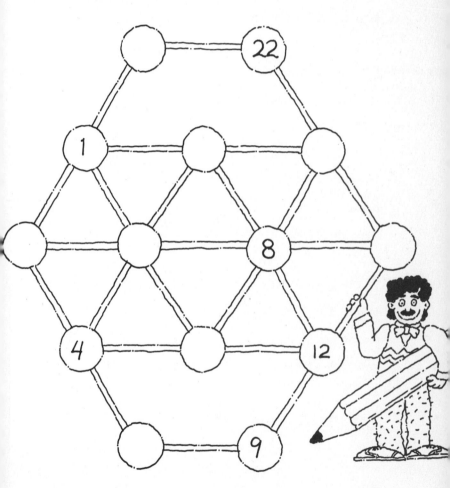

Humorous Bible Riddles

1. Why was Moses the most wicked man who ever lived?

   Broke all Commandments at once.

2. When was baseball first mentioned in the Bible?

   In the big - inning

3. Who was the most popular actor in the Bible?

   Samson

4. Who was the fastest runner in the Bible?

   _____

5. Why was Adam's first day the longest?

   _____

6. What man in the Bible had no parents?

   _____

7. When was the apostle Paul a baker?

   _____

8. Why does the Bible tell us to love both our neighbors and our
   enemies?

   _____

9. When was the first mention of automobiles in the Bible?

   _____

10. What was Eve's telephone number in the Garden of Eden?

   _____

Kings for the Scholar

See if you can match each king with the number of years that he reigned.

1. Jeroboam (Son of Nebat)

2. Nadab

3. Baasha

4. Elah

5. Zimri

6. Omri

7. Ahab

8. Ahaziah

9. Jehoram

10. Jehu

11. Jehoahaz

12. Jehoash

13. Jeroboam (Son of Joash)

14. Zachariah

15. Shallum

16. Menahem

17. Pekahiah

18. Pekah

19. Hoshea

A. 22 years

B. 17 years

C. 2 years

D. 41 years

E. 12 years

F. 10 years

G. 24 years

H. 28 years

I. 16 years

J. 7 days

K. 1 month

L. 6 months

M. 9 years

N. 20 years

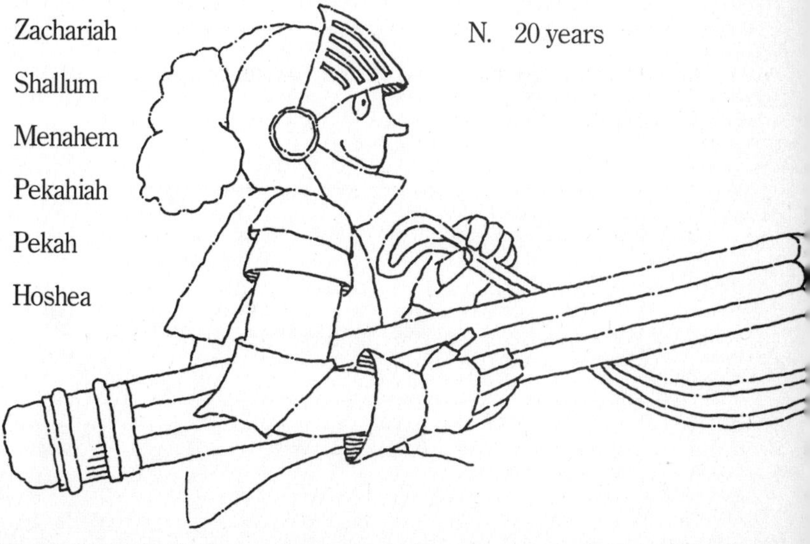

Priscilla's Problem

Help Priscilla place the lettered pieces into the empty diagram below. If placed correctly, 20 five-letter words will be formed. The words can be read by reading across the tops and bottoms of the pieces, and by reading down the left and right sides of the pieces. The arrows indicate where each word begins.

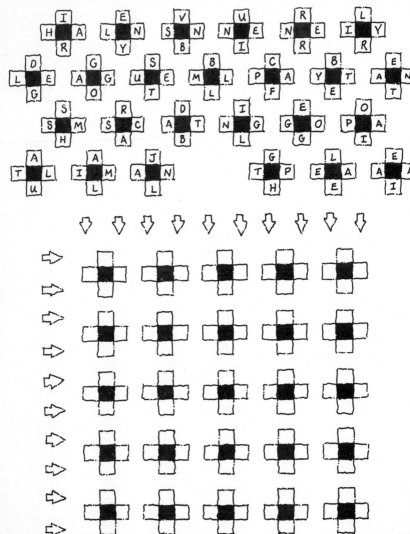

Jumbles

For both of the jumbles below, unscramble the names of four men mentioned in the Bible. Write these names on the blanks to the right. The letters in the parentheses now form a new scrambled name. Write these letters on the blanks provided. Now unscramble this name

SCRAMBLED NAME   UNSCRAMBLED NAME

1. H S E P J O   __ (__) __ __ __ (__)

   H L I A T G O   __ __ (__) (__) __ __ __

   P M E H R I A   __ (__) __ __ __ __ (__)

   N E A R   (__) __ __ (__)

   New scrambled name   (__) (__) (__) (__) (__) (__) (__) (__)

   Unscrambled name   __ __ __ __ __ __ __ __

2. E E E E B D Z   (__) __ __ __ __ __ __

   N E B U E R   (__) __ (__) __ __ __

   U A S L   (__) __ __ (__)

   A C A A N N   __ __ __ (__) (__) __

   New scrambled name   (__) (__) (__) (__) (__) (__) (__)

   Unscrambled name   __ __ __ __ __ __ __

The Ten Commandments

See if you can unroll the scroll of the Ten Commandments and complete each of the sentences.

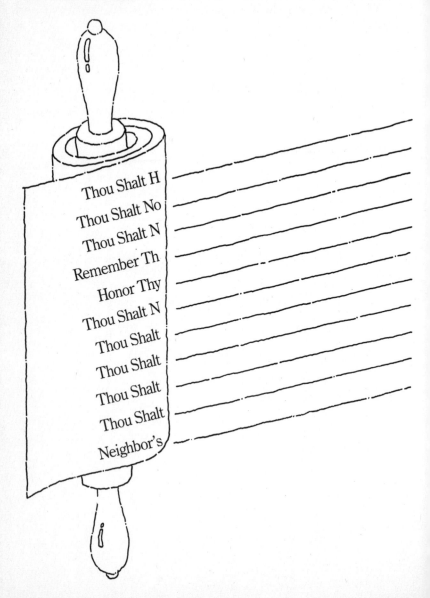

Thou Shalt H

Thou Shalt No

Thou Shalt N

Remember Th

Honor Thy

Thou Shalt N

Thou Shalt

Thou Shalt

Thou Shalt

Thou Shalt

Neighbor's

Bible Occupations

In the following word hunt see if you can find 37 occupations mentioned in the Bible. Begin with any letter and move one letter at a time to the right, left, up, down, or diagonally. When you have found a word, draw a circle around it.

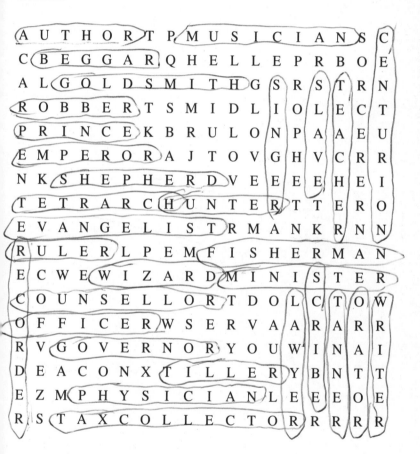

```
A U T H O R T P M U S I C I A N S C
C B E G G A R Q H E L L E P R B O E
A L G O L D S M I T H G S R S T R N
R O B B E R T S M I D L I O L E C T
P R I N C E K B R U L O N P A A E U
E M P E R O R A J T O V G H V C R R
N K S H E P H E R D V E E E H E I
T E T R A R C H U N T E R T T E R O
E V A N G E L I S T R M A N K R N N
R U L E R L P E M F I S H E R M A N
E C W E W I Z A R D M I N I S T E R
C O U N S E L L O R T D O L C T O W
O F F I C E R W S E R V A A R A R R
R V G O V E R N O R Y O U W I N A I
D E A C O N X T I L L E R Y B N T T
E Z M P H Y S I C I A N L E E E O E
R S T A X C O L L E C T O R R R R R
```

31

The Good Samaritan

Help the Good Samaritan find his way to the Inn.

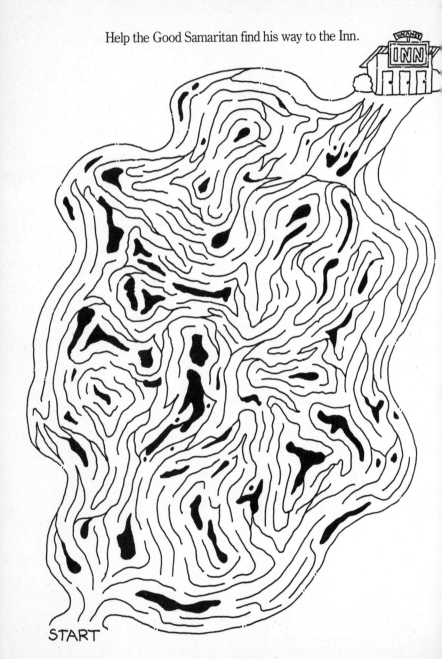

INN

START

Name the Event

The picture below illustrates a Bible event, story, or verse. See if you can guess which Bible event, story, or verse the picture is illustrating.

_____

_____

_____

_____

_____

Where in the Bible is this event, story, or verse found?

_____

Tail Tag

Begin at the top arrow and find a verse from the Bible. Move one square at a time to the right, left, up, down, or diagonally. End the verse at the bottom arrow.

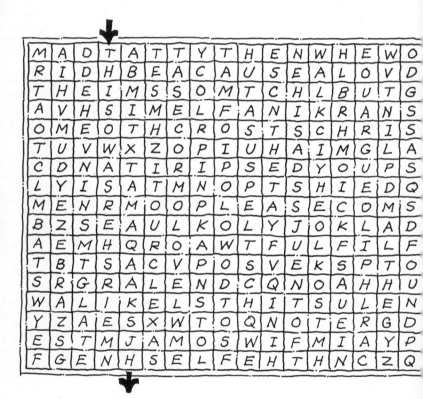

M	A	D	T	A	T	T	Y	T	H	E	N	W	H	E	W	O
R	I	D	H	B	E	A	C	A	U	S	E	A	L	O	V	D
T	H	E	I	M	S	S	O	M	T	C	H	L	B	U	T	G
A	V	H	S	I	M	E	L	F	A	N	I	K	R	A	N	S
O	M	E	O	T	H	C	R	O	S	T	S	C	H	R	I	S
T	U	V	W	X	Z	O	P	I	U	H	A	I	M	G	L	A
C	D	N	A	T	I	R	I	P	S	E	D	Y	O	U	P	S
L	Y	I	S	A	T	M	N	O	P	T	S	H	I	E	D	Q
M	E	N	R	M	O	O	P	L	E	A	S	E	C	O	M	S
B	Z	S	E	A	U	L	K	O	L	Y	J	O	K	L	A	D
A	E	M	H	Q	R	O	A	W	T	F	U	L	F	I	L	F
T	B	T	S	A	C	V	P	O	S	V	E	K	S	P	T	O
S	R	G	R	A	L	E	N	D	C	Q	N	O	A	H	H	U
W	A	L	I	K	E	L	S	T	H	I	T	S	U	L	E	N
Y	Z	A	E	S	X	W	T	O	Q	N	O	T	E	R	G	D
E	S	T	M	J	A	M	O	S	W	I	F	M	I	A	Y	P
F	G	E	N	H	S	E	L	F	E	H	T	H	N	C	Z	Q

34

Vocation Match

See if you can match the names of Bible characters with their vocations.

1. Barak _____		A.	Inventor
2. Tertullus _____		B.	Shepherd
3. Asaph _____		C.	Slave
4. Barabbas _____		D.	Sorcerer
5. Lydia _____		E.	Lawyer
6. Gehazi _____		F.	Tentmaker
7. Abel _____		G.	Coppersmith
8. Tubal-cain _____		H.	Heretic
9. Onesimus _____		I.	Tanner
10. Simon _____		J.	Liberator
11. Zenas _____		K.	Orator
12. Aquila _____		L.	Musician
13. Alexander _____		M.	Robber
14. Philetus _____		N.	Saleswoman
15. Simon of Joppa _____		O.	Servant

Name the Event

The picture below illustrates a Bible event, story, or verse. See if you can guess which Bible event, story, or verse the picture is illustrating.

_____

_____

_____

_____

_____

Where in the Bible is this event, story, or verse found?

_____

A Special Place

In two moves, see if you can discover where Job lived.

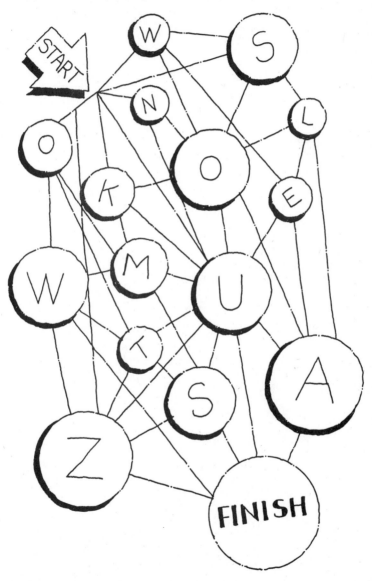

Guess Who

1. Who was a very fat man who was stabbed to death? _____

2. Who walked on water? _____

3. Who was also called Levi? _____

4. Who was also called Peter? _____

5. Who was with Jesus on the Mount of Transfiguration?

_____

6. Who turned Jesus over to the Jews to be crucified? _____

7. Who complained about all her housework? _____

8. Who went to Abraham's bosom? _____

9. Who was a publican? _____

10. Who was Mary and Martha's brother? _____

11. Who came to Jesus by night? _____

12. To whom did Luke write the Book of Acts? _____

13. Who was chosen as an apostle to replace Judas? _____

14. Who was killed for lying to the Holy Spirit? _____

15. Who said, "If it be of God, you cannot overthrow it"? _____

16. Who was the first Christian martyr? _____

17. Who talked to an Ethiopian? _____

18. Who was the Gentile that Peter visited? _____

19. Who wrote the Book of Romans for the apostle Paul? _____

20. Who had a servant named Onesimus? _____

Patchword

This patchwork-quilt diagram contains ten Bible words or names all mixed up. Three patches form one word — use each patch only once. See if you can piece together the names and words and write them on the lines below.

1. _____   4. _____   7. _____

2. _____   5. _____   8. _____

3. _____   6. _____   9. _____

10. _____

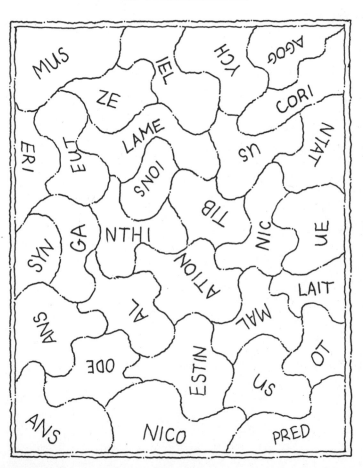

The Sons of Jacob

Match the sons of Jacob with their mothers:

1. Dan

2. Levi

3. Gad

4. Benjamin

5. Reuben

6. Zebulun

7. Naphtali

8. Simeon

9. Asher

10. Judah

11. Issachar

12. Joseph

Leah

Rachel

Bilhah

Zilpah

Fill in the missing part:

13. Jacob wrestled with a man who touched him where?

    _____

14. The man who wrestled with Jacob changed his name to what?

    _____

15. Jacob called the place where he wrestled with the man

    _____.

16. Jacob said, "I have seen _____ _____ to

    _____, and my life is preserved."

17. When Jacob met his brother Esau, how many men did Esau have

    with him? _____

18. Jacob had a daughter whose name was _____.

    A. Delilah   B. Dinah   C. Diana   D. Dara

19. Jacob's wife Rachel died at the birth of _____.

Patchword

This patchwork-quilt diagram contains ten Bible words or names all mixed up. Three patches form one word — use each patch only once. See if you can piece together the names and words and write them on the lines below.

1. _____   4. _____   7. _____

2. _____   5. _____   8. _____

3. _____   6. _____   9. _____

10. _____

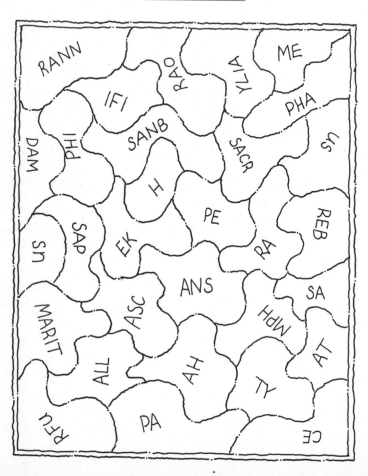

Hannah's Headache

Here is a word search with a twist. The word "Hannah" is hidden 31 separate times in the diagram below. Our expert found them in just three minutes. See if you can beat the expert.

H	A	N	N	A	H	A	N	N	A	H	A	A	H
N	H	A	H	A	N	N	A	H	H	A	A	A	N
H	A	A	A	H	A	N	N	H	A	N	N	A	H
H	A	N	N	A	H	N	N	H	A	N	N	A	H
A	H	A	N	N	A	H	A	A	A	A	N	H	H
N	H	N	A	H	A	N	N	A	H	H	A	A	A
N	A	N	H	A	N	H	H	A	N	N	A	H
A	N	A	N	A	H	H	A	A	H	N	A	H	H
H	N	H	H	N	H	A	N	N	A	H	H	H	A
A	A	A	A	A	H	N	N	H	N	A	H	A	N
N	H	N	N	A	H	N	A	A	N	A	A	N	N
H	A	N	N	A	H	A	H	N	A	H	H	N	A
N	A	A	A	A	A	H	A	N	H	A	H	A	H
H	A	H	H	N	H	H	H	A	N	N	A	H	H

Peter's Path

Follow one continuous winding path to find a quote from Peter. The quote is found in 2 Peter 3:18. Start with the letter "B" and end with the letter "N." Each new word starts with one of the circled letters. The last letter of one word is next to the circled first letter of the next word. The number of letters in each word in the quotation is given below the answer blanks at the bottom of the page.

```
L O R D R A N G E L S T O O (N) H T O (B) Y R U N
N M E (A) E V E S A T A N W I (B) E (G) L O R O U T
S E M A E I R O (F) D N (A) T O M I (H) O (T) C A R E
A R E Y O U H A V I N G F U N Y E T O T H I M
H E L L O R (L) S M I L E (S) A V I O L O S I R H
T H I S U U O C D (A) N D H O U S E R C A R E (C)
I S A H A (O) R R D O N N (I) D N (A) E S (J) E S U S
L I P (O) F U N (K) H I (T) K S C E E M Y J N A M E
T O E S K Y N O E H I P A L O O K I S R B O B
O G M A N O N A L L M E R S N (I) W O R (G) F U N
D D E L W H H I R I D E S (G) S I T O J T U S U
D O S Y O U M L I K E K P U Z Z E L S L M (B) O
```

___ ___ ___ ___ ___ ___ ___
 3   4   2   5   3   2   3

___ ___ ___ ___ ___ ___
  9   2   3   4   3   6

___ ___ . ___ ___ ___ ___ ___
 5   6   2   3   2   5   4

___ ___ ___ ___ . ___ .
 3   3   3   4   4

44

Quotation Puzzle

In the puzzle below, fit the letters of each column into the boxes directly above them. The letters may or may not go into the boxes in the same order in which they are listed. It is up to you to decide which letter goes into which box. Once a letter is used, cross it off the bottom half of the diagram and do not use it again. Some letters have been entered into boxes to help you get started, and those letters have been crossed off. Black squares are used to separate the words of the quotation. When the diagram is filled in, you will find the completed quotation by reading the boxes horizontally.

Bible Labyrinth

Hidden in the following Bible labyrinth is a verse from the Bible. Start at the top arrow and move one space at a time to the right, left, up, or down. You should finish the verse at the side arrow.

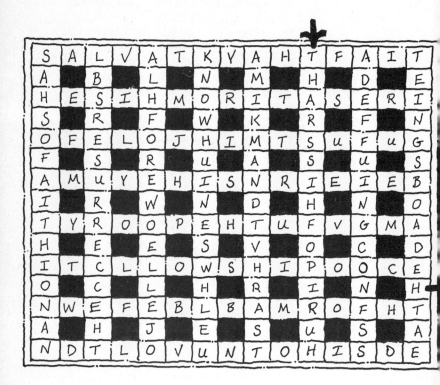

Names and Meanings Match

See if you can match the names of Bible characters with the meanings of their names.

1. Eli _____
2. Elijah _____
3. Emmanuel _____
4. Eve _____
5. Jacob _____
6. Jesus _____
7. Paul _____
8. Peter _____
9. Philip _____
10. Satan _____
11. Solomon _____
12. Joshua _____
13. Moses _____
14. Naomi _____
15. Theophilus _____

A. Adversary
B. Little
C. A stone
D. My God is Jehovah
E. Pleasant
F. Life
G. God with us
H. Supplanter

I. Loved of God
J. My God
K. Saved from the water
L. Peaceful
M. Lover of horses
N. Jehovah is salvation
O. Savior

Quotation Puzzle

In the puzzle below, fit the letters of each column into the boxes directly above them. The letters may or may not go into the boxes in the same order in which they are listed. It is up to you to decide which letter goes into which box. Once a letter is used, cross it off the bottom half of the diagram and do not use it again. Some letters have been entered into boxes to help you get started, and those letters have been crossed off. Black squares are used to separate the words of the quotation. When the diagram is filled in, you will find the completed quotation by reading the boxes horizontally.

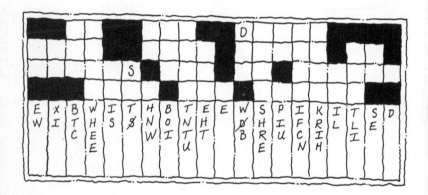

Key Word

To find the key word, fill in the blanks in words 1 through 10 with the correct missing letters. Transfer those letters to the correspondingly numbered squares in the diagram.

1. A L _ H A
2. N I L _
3. P A R _ N
4. _ H I L D
5. B _ D

6. A _ E N
7. M _ G I
8. _ I N G
9. P O _ T
10. B _ A S S

1	2	3	4	5	6	7	8	9	10

Alphabet Fill-in

The 26 letters of the alphabet are missing from the puzzle below. See if you can place them where they belong. You can cross the letters off as you use them.

A B C D E F G H I J K L M

N O P Q R S T U V W X Y Z

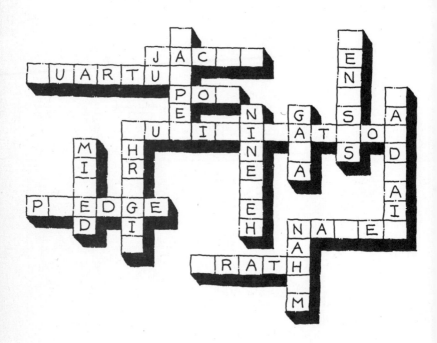

Son Rays

See if you can identify 12 different names for Jesus
that fit in the puzzle below.

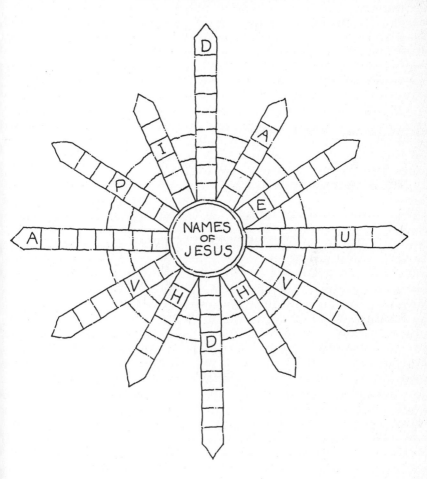

Who Said It?

See if you can identify who said the following quotes: Peter, James, John, Jesus, Paul, Jeremiah, or God.

1. "The heart is deceitful above all things . . . ."

   _____

2. "God shall wipe away all tears from their eyes."

   _____

3. "Ephraim is joined to idols."

   _____

4. "Perfect love casteth out fear."

   _____

5. "Can two walk together, except they be agreed?"

   _____

6. "Love covers over a multitude of sins" (NIV).

   _____

7. "Even Solomon in all his glory was not arrayed like one of these."

   _____

8. "I will show thee my faith by my works."

   _____

9. "Prove all things; hold fast that which is good."

   _____

10. "Godliness with contentment is great gain."

   _____

Pharaoh's Diamond

Enter Pharaoh's hall of rooms and see if you can find your way to the diamond.

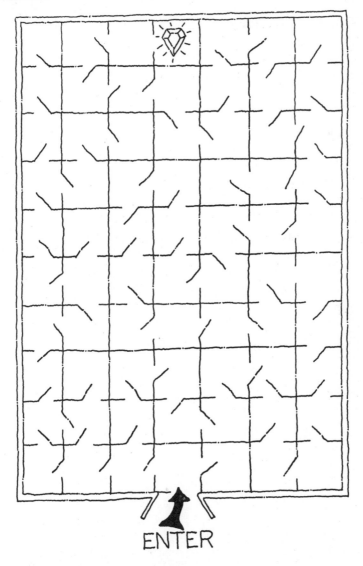

ENTER

Bible Anagram

For each description below, write the name of the person in the blanks provided. The first letters of the 14 names spell the name of a proud, imperious king. The position of the letter in the king's name is included under each blank.

1. The name of Saul's uncle.

    __ __ __
    9 10 14

2. A godly scribe.

    __ __ __ __
    10 11 14 13

3. A city of refuge.

    __ __ __ __ __
    3 2 11 10 14

4. The dwelling place of a patriarch.

    __ __
    4 11

5. A town in Galilee.

    __ __ __ __
    5 7 9 13

6. A friend of Moses.

    __ __ __
    6 4 14

7. A river of Damascus.

    __ __ __ __ __
    7 3 13 9 7

8. A tribe of Israel.

    __ __ __
    8 7 9

9. The father of a general.

    __ __ __
    1 4 9

10. A judge of Israel.

    __ __ __ __
    2 6 4 8

11. A prince slain at a winepress.

    __ __ __ __
    11 10 2 3

12. A king of Midian.

    __ __ __ __ __
    11 10 3 7 6

13. A warrior.

    __ __ __ __ __
    13 3 1 2 14

14. A son of Jacob.

    __ __ __ __ __ __
    14 10 4 3 2 1

Quotation Puzzle

In the puzzle below, fit the letters of each column into the boxes directly above them. The letters may or may not go into the boxes in the same order in which they are listed. It is up to you to decide which letter goes into which box. Once a letter is used, cross it off the bottom half of the diagram and do not use it again. Some letters have been entered into boxes to help you get started, and those letters have been crossed off. Black squares are used to separate the words of the quotation. When the diagram is filled in, you will find the completed quotation by reading the boxes horizontally.

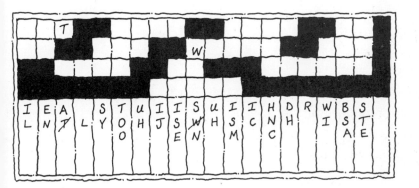

Jumbles

For both of the jumbles below, unscramble the names of four men
mentioned in the Bible. Write these names on the blanks to the right. The
letters in the parentheses now form a new scrambled name. Write these
letters on the blanks provided. Now unscramble this name.

SCRAMBLED NAME	UNSCRAMBLED NAME
1. V D I A D	(__) __ __ (__) __
B J O	__ (__) (__)
A D N	__ (__) __
A A H M N	(__) __ __ (__) __
New scrambled name	(__) (__) (__) (__) (__) (__) (__
Unscrambled name	__ __ __ __ __ __ __

2. A P E P A R H S	(__) __ __ __ __ (__) __ (__)
B C E A L	(__) __ (__) __ __
E D G I O N	__ (__) __ __ (__) __
A N H U M	(__) __ __ (__) __

New scrambled name

(__) (__) (__) (__) (__) (__) (__) (__) (__)

Unscrambled name

__ __ __ __ __ __ __ __ __ __

56

Quotation Puzzle

In the puzzle below, fit the letters of each column into the boxes directly above them. The letters may or may not go into the boxes in the same order in which they are listed. It is up to you to decide which letter goes into which box. Once a letter is used, cross it off the bottom half of the diagram and do not use it again. Some letters have been entered into boxes to help you get started, and those letters have been crossed off. Black squares are used to separate the words of the quotation. When the diagram is filled in, you will find the completed quotation by reading the boxes horizontally.

Syl-La-Puzzle

See if you can identify 20 Bible words or names of people by using all the syllables in the Syllabox. The number of syllables to be used in each answer is shown in parentheses. The number of letters in each answer is indicated by the blank spaces. Each syllable will be used only once.

Syllabox

A AE AEL AH AH BA BAR BER CHIZ CLE CO CON CRITE DE
DEEM DEK DEM DI DI E E ER GEL HEM HY I IST LA
MEL MENT NA NA NAZ NI NE O O OINT PENT PLE PO RE
RE RETH RUS SAL SCI SHIP SION TA THAN THY TIM
TIM TION TIONS US US VA VAN VER VO WOR ZA

1. False   (3) __ __ __ __ __ __ __ __
2. Follower   (3) __ __ __ __ __ __ __ __
3. Lotion   (2) __ __ __ __ __ __ __
4. Dwelling   (4) __ __ __ __ __ __ __ __ __
5. Experience   (3) __ __ __ __ __ __ __ __ __
6. Study   (3) __ __ __ __ __ __ __ __
7. Turn   (2) __ __ __ __ __ __
8. Adoration   (2) __ __ __ __ __ __ __
9. Proclaim   (4) __ __ __ __ __ __ __ __ __
10. By night   (4) __ __ __ __ __ __ __ __
11. Under a tree   (3) __ __ __ __ __ __ __ __
12. Prophet   (4) __ __ __ __ __ __
13. Dead   (3) __ __ __ __ __ __
14. Young man   (3) __ __ __ __ __ __
15. Savior   (3) __ __ __ __ __ __
16. Priest   (4) __ __ __ __ __ __ __ __ __ __
17. Wall builder   (4) __ __ __ __ __ __ __
18. Blind   (4) __ __ __ __ __ __ __ __ __
19. Rescue   (3) __ __ __ __ __ __ __ __
20. Birthplace   (3) __ __ __ __ __ __ __

Tail Tag

Begin at the top arrow and see if you can find a verse from the Bible. Move one square at a time to the right, left, up, down, or diagonally. End the verse at the bottom arrow.

A	C	I	T	M	N	L	I	G	H	W	E	E	S	T	E	L
B	M	O	P	R	S	E	A	J	B	O	B	I	N	A	I	S
S	U	R	E	B	E	E	T	S	S	A	M	C	O	L	A	T
P	L	U	Q	S	S	E	N	R	E	T	T	I	B	L	W	I
H	I	T	M	A	E	T	W	I	C	E	H	O	P	E	L	L
J	U	M	P	N	T	R	U	C	K	I	N	M	E	L	B	A
G	K	I	M	D	W	R	A	T	H	A	N	D	L	I	S	O
B	N	D	F	G	Q	H	O	C	H	R	I	A	S	T	Y	V
E	P	I	H	W	X	Y	Z	Y	O	N	E	N	E	I	D	O
P	H	O	K	P	S	E	O	N	E	M	W	G	O	N	C	P
U	S	T	M	A	E	L	S	A	T	P	U	E	A	J	L	K
T	A	W	A	Y	E	P	M	W	R	S	V	R	B	L	A	R
S	U	Q	P	F	O	P	A	N	J	A	M	E	S	M	M	S
A	W	O	I	R	F	N	S	C	H	R	I	S	P	Q	O	T
E	I	B	Y	O	D	C	D	L	I	V	E	D	N	A	R	H
D	T	X	A	M	B	O	B	L	O	V	E	S	O	C	U	T
C	H	A	L	L	M	A	L	I	C	E	S	P	A	M	E	I

Choose-A-Letter

To discover the Bible verse concealed in the diagram below you will have
to choose letters. Choose one letter in each pair and draw a line through
the other one. Then read across the remaining letters of each row to find
the words in a familiar Bible verse.

_____

_____

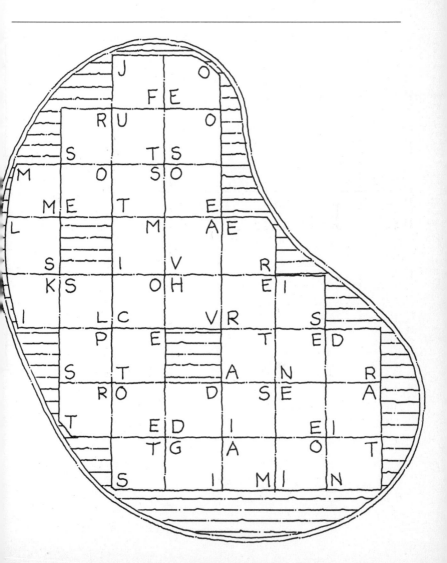

Quotation Puzzle

In the puzzle below, fit the letters of each column into the boxes directly above them. The letters may or may not go into the boxes in the same order in which they are listed. It is up to you to decide which letter goes into which box. Once a letter is used, cross it off the bottom half of the diagram and do not use it again. Some letters have been entered into boxes to help you get started, and those letters have been crossed off. Black squares are used to separate the words of the quotation. When the diagram is filled in, you will find the completed quotation by reading the boxes horizontally.

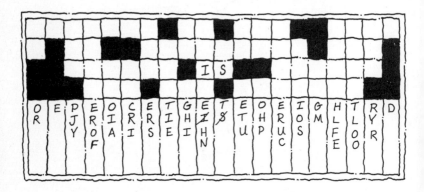

Name the Event

The picture below illustrates a Bible event, story, or verse. See if you can guess which Bible event, story, or verse the picture is illustrating.

_____

_____

_____

_____

_____

Where in the Bible is this event, story, or verse found?

_____

Alphagram

Twenty-six words from the Bible are hidden in the diagram on the opposite page. See if you can find them all. There is one word in each row, and one letter is missing from each word. The missing letter may be at the beginning, end, or anyplace within the word. As you fill in the diagram you will find that there are 26 missing letters — one letter for each letter of the alphabet. Since a letter will be used only once, an alphabetical listing has been provided for your assistance. As you use a letter in the diagram, cross it off the alphabetical list.

A B C D E F G H I
J K L M N O P Q R
S T U V W X Y Z

A	C	O	A	T		U	T	S	T	M
P	A	T	R	I		R	C	H	U	J
X	D	V	W	E		I	L	E	B	S
E	M	A	R	A		A	T	H	A	T
V	A	F	N	G		U	A	I	L	S
Q	O	P	R	O		E	R	B	S	Z
W	X	C	O	R		N	T	H	Q	H
P	R	A	Y	E		D	F	S	U	L
A	P	R	C	N		M	B	E	R	S
Y	H	Q	L	A		A	R	U	S	K
W	B	L	A	M		E	E	R	P	S
C	P	F	O	M		G	A	O	K	L
Z	S	A	M	S		N	E	S	R	T
X	T	N	G	W		O	G	O	S	M
A	D	M	O	R		E	C	A	I	F
J	M	I	M	U		I	C	E	P	N
D	X	B	M	A		I	D	C	O	P
L	R	H	L	A		E	S	S	R	M
B	P	Y	R	A		I	D	S	B	R
C	K	I	E	G		P	T	N	H	S
L	H	A	J	K		H	I	L	I	P
I	L	E	V	I		E	S	C	T	S
J	D	I	H	L		R	O	S	S	U
E	M	L	T	D		A	D	E	S	H
G	F	J	A	E		L	O	O	D	M
K	M	J	R	F		U	D	G	E	S

Patchword

This patchwork-quilt diagram contains 15 Bible words or names all mixed up. Two patches form one word — use each patch only once. See if you can piece together the names and words and write them on the lines below.

1. _____   6. _____   11. _____

2. _____   7. _____   12. _____

3. _____   8. _____   13. _____

4. _____   9. _____   14. _____

5. _____   10. _____   15. _____

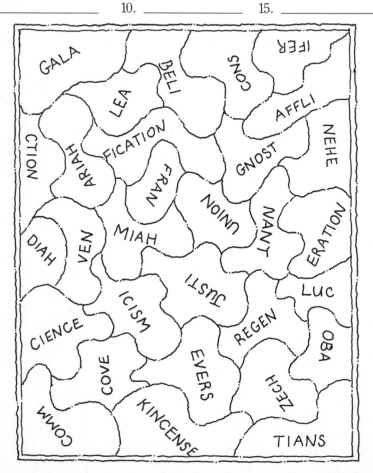

Jumbles

For both of the jumbles below, unscramble the names of four men mentioned in the Bible. Write these names on the blanks to the right. The letters in the parentheses now form a new scrambled name. Write these letters on the blanks provided. Now unscramble this name.

SCRAMBLED NAME   UNSCRAMBLED NAME

1. W T T H M A E   __ (__) (__) __ (__) (__) __

   F X I L E   __ (__) (__) __ __

   H U D E   __ (__) (__) __

   S A M D E   __ __ (__) __ (__)

New scrambled name

(__) (__) (__) (__) (__) (__) (__) (__) (__) (__)

Unscrambled name

__ __ __ __ __ __ __ __ __ __

2. S I T U T   (__) __ __ __ (__)

   D H R E O   __ (__) __ __ __

   O A N H   (__) __ __ (__)

   E T R P E   (__) __ __ (__) __

New scrambled name   (__) (__) (__) (__) (__) (__) (__)

Unscrambled name   __ __ __ __ __ __ __

Find the Angel

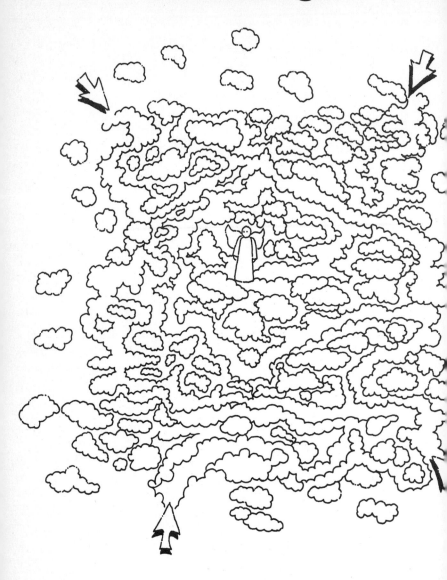

Who Said It?

All of the following quotes can be attributed to one of the three men listed below. See if you can guess "Who said it?"

JOSEPH   MOSES   ELIJAH

1. "I seek my brethren."_____

2. "There shall not be dew nor rain these years."_____

3. "The birds shall eat thy flesh from off thee."_____

4. "The Lord hath not appeared unto thee."_____

5. "Take away my life for I am not better than my fathers."_____

6. "Show me Thy glory."_____

7. "Come near unto me."_____

8. "How can I do this great wickedness...against God?"_____

9. "As an eagle stirreth up her nest..."_____

10. "Prepare thy chariot, and get thee down."_____

11. "Look out a man discreet and wise."_____

12. "If the Lord be God, follow him."_____

13. "God is come to prove you."_____

14. "Fear not: for am I in the place of God?"_____

15. "Fear ye not, stand still, and see the salvation of the Lord."_____

Alphabet Fill-in

The 26 letters of the alphabet are missing from the puzzle below. See if you can place them where they belong. You can cross the letters off as you use them.

A B C D E F G H I J K L M
N O P Q R S T U V W X Y Z

Something Noah Found

Start at the arrow and move one square at a time in any direction. You may move to the right, left, up, down, or diagonally, but do not cross any letter twice. All the letters must be used to discover what Noah found.

N	O	F	E	I	T	E	Y
A	H	O	C	N	E	H	E
D	U	A	R	L	E	F	S
N	G	R	O	D	H	T	O

_____

_____

_____

Key Word

To find the key word, fill in the blanks in words 1 through 10 with the correct missing letters. Transfer those letters to the correspondingly numbered squares in the diagram.

1. A G A __ E

2. A G __

3. G E __ T I L E

4. S __ E P H E N

5. __ C H A N

6. P R O P H E __

7. D A N I __ L

8. __ N C L E

9. S __ O R P I O N

10. A __ A B

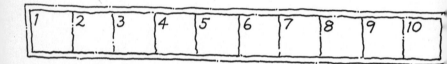

1	2	3	4	5	6	7	8	9	10

Name the Event

The picture below illustrates a Bible event, story, or verse. See if you can guess which Bible event, story, or verse the picture is illustrating.

_____

_____

_____

_____

Where in the Bible is this event, story, or verse found?

_____

Bishops and Deacons

In 1 Timothy 3:2-12 are listed the qualifications of bishops and deacons. How many can you remember?

1. _____

2. _____

3. _____

4. _____

5. _____

6. _____

7. _____

8. _____

9. _____

10. _____

11. _____

12. _____

13. _____

14. _____

15. _____

16. _____

17. _____

18. _____

Old Testament Characters

The letters in the following columns go into the boxes directly below them, but in a different order. When the letters are correctly placed they will spell the names of eight Old Testament characters. (Not all of the letters in each column are used.)

J	I	D	E	O	E	S	L	R	H	H	E
J	A	L	O	H	N	E	A	O	A	O	L
G	O	C	F	B	S	E	N	O	T	S	R
C	A	B	E	B	A	G	S	T	C	R	D

Who Said It?

See if you can identify who said the following quotes: Moses, Samuel, Balaam, Abraham, Job, God, or the Queen of Sheba.

1. "The imagination of man's heart is evil from his youth."

   _____

2. "Shall not the Judge of all the earth do right?"

   _____

3. "Eye for eye, tooth for tooth..."

   _____

4. "Love thy neighbor as thyself."

   _____

5. "Let me die the death of the righteous."

   _____

6. "Be sure your sin will find you out."

   _____

7. "...the apple of his eye."

   _____

8. "A man after his own heart..."

   _____

9. "The half was not told me."

   _____

10. "Man is born to trouble, as the sparks fly upward."

    _____

A Place for Everyone

Can you find a place for every one of the four-letter names of Bible characters listed below? One individual has already been given a place. Use each name only once.

ABDA	BOAZ	EZRA	NAUM
ABEL	CAIN	GAAL	NEBO
ADAM	CORE	GERA	NERI
AGEE	~~DODO~~	HAZO	OBED
AMOS	EBER	HELI	OMAR
ANAK	ELON	IRAD	REBA
AZOR	ENAN	KORE	UZZA
BELA	ESAU	LAEL	ZINA
BEOR			

Famous Prisoners

How many famous prisoners of the Bible can you name?

1. _____

2. _____

3. _____

4. _____

5. _____

6. _____

7. _____

8. _____

9. _____

10. _____

11. _____

12. _____

13. _____

14. _____

Bible Labyrinth

Hidden in the following Bible labyrinth is a verse from the Bible. Start at the top arrow and move one space at a time to the right, left, up, or down. You should finish the verse at the bottom arrow.

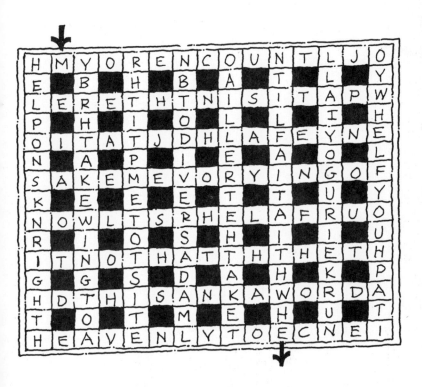

Guess Who

1. Who was the prophet that predicted where the Messiah was to be born?_____

2. Who wrote the last book in the Old Testament?_____

3. Who ripped off the gates of a city?_____

4. Who said, "Thy people shall be my people, and thy God my God"?

   _____

5. Who was the priest that had evil sons?_____

6. Who cut Samson's hair?_____

7. Who became the second husband of Ruth?_____

8. Who was Israel's first king?_____

9. Who was the prophet who denounced King Saul?_____

10. Who was David's best friend?_____

11. Who was David's first wife?_____

12. Who had lame feet?_____

13. Who did King David have killed?_____

14. Who was hung in a tree by his head?_____

15. Who was fed by the ravens?_____

16. Who wanted Naboth's vineyard?_____

17. Who was partly eaten by dogs?_____

18. Who walked with God?_____

19. Who dipped himself in the Jordan River seven times?_____

20. Who built the temple?_____

Who Wrote Romans?

In seven moves, see if you can discover who wrote the Book of Romans for the apostle Paul.

Versigram

Unscramble the following familiar Bible verses.

1. hTe orLd lsao ilwl eb a ergefu orf hte prsesopde, a

   _____

   gefuer ni imtse fo uortelb.

   _____

2. oFr vene hte oSn fo nam meca otn ot eb nitsimrede

   _____

   ntuo, tub ot nitsimre, nda ot veig ihs file a nsarmo

   _____

   ofr ynma.

   _____

3. hTe rahte si ticefedlu voabe lal nihgst, nda psraeetedyl

   _____

   kceiwd; how nac kwon ti?

   _____

4. nAd ti lahls moec ot saps, hatt soeohwrev hlals lcal

   _____

   no hte mane fo hte roLd lahls eb vesad.

   _____

5. oT na hrienicneat rorutcpnilbei, nda feidlendu, nda

   _____

   atht edatfh otn waya, srerevde ni vahene ofr uoy.

   _____

Mixed Letters

Rearrange the letters to find out who said, "Can there any good thing come out of Nazareth?"

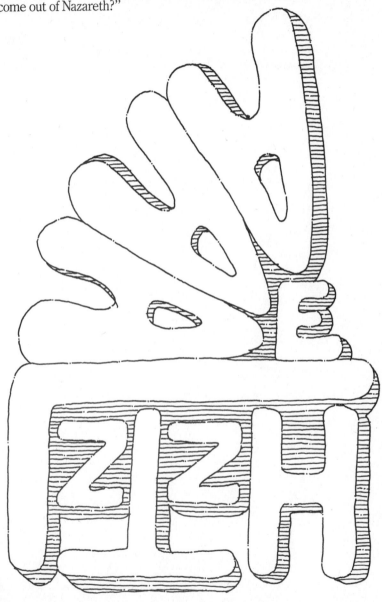

Jumbles

For both of the jumbles below, unscramble the names of four men mentioned in the Bible. Write these names on the blanks to the right. The letters in the parentheses now form a new scrambled name. Write these letters on the blanks provided. Now unscramble this name.

SCRAMBLED NAME   UNSCRAMBLED NAME

1. R A N A O   __ (__) __ __ __

   N A A C H   __ __ (__) __ __

   W R E N A D   __ __ __ (__) (__) __

   B G A U S A   __ __ __ __ __ (__)

   New scrambled name   (__) (__) (__) (__) (__)

   Unscrambled name   __ __ __ __ __

2. X X T A R A E E S __ __ __ __ (__) (__) (__) __ __

   M A L A E K   (__) __ __ (__) (__) __

   M D A A   __ (__) __ __

   K N A A   (__) (__) __ __

   New scrambled name (__) (__) (__) (__) (__) (__) (__) (__) (__)

   Unscrambled name   __ __ __ __ __ __ __ __ __

84

Alphanumber

In the diagram below there are various numbers in each square. The numbers represent letters of the alphabet. Change the numbers to letters and discover an important Bible thought.

A	B	C	D	E	F	G	H	I	J	K	L	M	N
1	2	3	4	5	6	7	8	9	10	11	12	13	14

O	P	Q	R	S	T	U	V	W	X	Y	Z
15	16	17	18	19	20	21	22	23	24	25	26	27

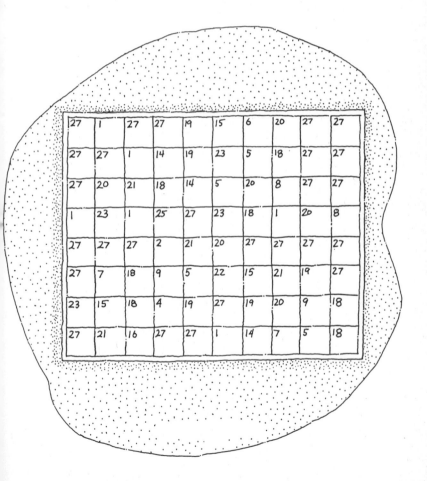

27	1	27	27	19	15	6	20	27	27
27	27	1	14	19	23	5	18	27	27
27	20	21	18	14	5	20	8	27	27
1	23	1	25	27	23	18	1	20	8
27	27	27	2	21	20	27	27	27	27
27	7	18	9	5	22	15	21	19	27
23	15	18	4	19	27	19	20	9	18
27	21	16	27	27	1	14	7	5	18

Key Word

To find the key word, fill in the blanks in words 1 through 10 with the correct missing letters. Transfer those letters to the correspondingly numbered squares in the diagram.

1. A L __ A R

2. __ M M O N

3. A __ E L

4. __ N O S H

5. A A __ O N

6. D A T H A __

7. L __ W

8. __ H E R U B

9. F E __ I X

10. B R __ A D

1	2	3	4	5	6	7	8	9	10

Humorous Bible Riddles

1. How did Jonah feel when the great fish swallowed him?_____
   _____

2. When did Moses sleep with five people in one bed?_____
   _____

3. What did Adam and Eve do when they were expelled from Eden?
   _____

4. Where was Solomon's temple located?_____

5. When Eve asked, "Adam, do you love me?" what was his reply?
   _____

6. Why did Moses cross the Red Sea?_____

7. Who was the most successful physician in the Bible?_____

8. Who was the straightest man in the Bible?_____

9. Where is tennis mentioned in the Bible?_____
   _____

10. Where is deviled ham mentioned in the Bible?_____
    _____

Patchword

This patchwork-quilt diagram contains ten Bible words or names all mixed up. Three patches form one word — use each patch only once. See if you can piece together the names and words and write them on the lines below.

1. _____   4. _____   7. _____

2. _____   5. _____   8. _____

3. _____   6. _____   9. _____

10. _____

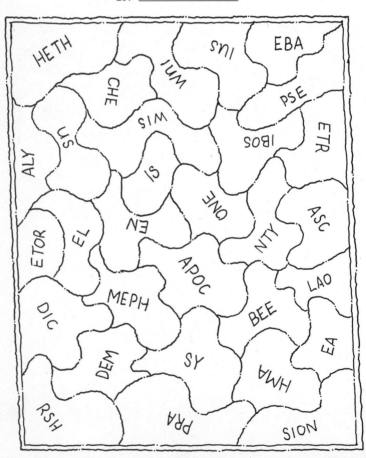

Quotation Puzzle

In the puzzle below, fit the letters of each column into the boxes directly above them. The letters may or may not go into the boxes in the same order in which they are listed. It is up to you to decide which letter goes into which box. Once a letter is used, cross it off the bottom half of the diagram and do not use it again. Some letters have been entered into boxes to help you get started, and those letters have been crossed off. Black squares are used to separate the words of the quotation. When the diagram is filled in, you will find the completed quotation by reading the boxes horizontally.

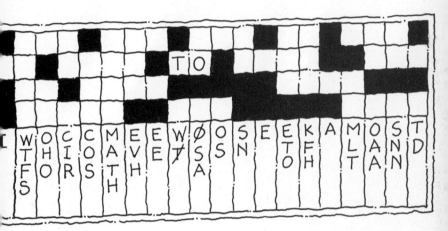

Bartimaeus' Bubbles

Help blind Bartimaeus through the bubble maze without bursting a bubble.

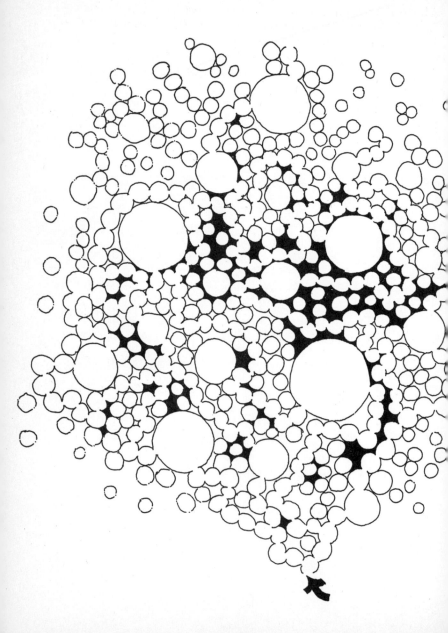

Lipogram

A lipogram is writing that avoids the use of particular letters. The following is an example: ch____ch = church. See if you can guess which letters are missing in the following lipogram Bible verses.

1. F____ wi____h ____d n__th__ng __h__l __e

   __m____ss__b__e.

2. __n ____e __e__in_____ng __o__ _____at____ __h__

   __ea__e__ a____ __h__ __ar__h.

3. A__ n__wbo__n __abes, ____sire the __in__er__ mil__

   of the _____d, __hat ye ____y __ro__ th____e__y.

4. Fo__ I am ____t __sh__me__ of the __o__p____ of

   __hr__s__: fo__ it is ____e __ow__r of ____d unto

   __al____tion to __v__r__ o__e that __eli__v__th; __o

   t__e ____w fi__st, an__ ____so to th__ ____ee__.

5. Ble____ed is the __an th__t w____keth not __n the

   __ou__sel of the un__od__y, __or s__an__eth in ____e

   __ay of s__nn__rs, nor s__tt__th in the _____t of

   t____ __c____n__ul. __ut ____s ____li____t is in

   ____e __a__ __f ____e __or__; a__d i__ his ____w

   __ot__ he ____d__ta__e ____y and ____gh__.

Name the Event

The picture below illustrates a Bible event, story, or verse. See if you can guess which Bible event, story, or verse the picture is illustrating.

_____

_____

_____

_____

_____

Where in the Bible is this event, story, or verse found?

_____

Tail Tag

Begin at the top arrow and see if you can find a verse from the Bible. Move one square at a time to the right, left, up, down, or diagonally. End the verse at the bottom arrow.

G	R	E	A	S	T	H	K	J	I	E	R	T	Y	O	A	E
L	J	H	M	A	H	S	E	B	S	T	A	I	M	P	L	I
C	M	O	H	T	S	I	A	L	W	U	I	S	X	Z	M	N
L	P	T	F	O	R	T	H	I	O	E	V	W	I	P	I	E
H	E	H	Z	N	Q	D	S	R	T	H	U	K	A	N	R	A
D	K	L	M	P	H	T	N	Q	N	H	T	I	L	T	N	O
Y	I	K	J	A	V	U	R	A	O	M	J	S	M	H	W	R
U	S	A	T	X	W	E	I	P	T	H	G	I	L	E	T	S
R	I	E	P	L	H	F	S	I	N	R	E	S	J	R	Q	P
A	T	N	M	T	R	I	D	C	D	A	R	K	N	E	S	S
H	O	A	O	M	D	N	A	R	G	B	O	B	Z	Y	U	E
H	Z	R	J	O	N	Y	T	S	I	R	H	C	K	I	O	V
I	B	F	Y	R	S	Z	E	R	A	S	B	Q	P	A	I	E
S	A	O	P	I	D	A	D	P	Y	Z	L	I	T	N	U	N
I	L	R	A	E	S	R	N	L	Q	H	N	S	M	Y	M	S
V	T	A	E	R	G	E	U	R	S	I	O	T	I	M	E	Q
G	O	H	V	T	P	U	T	S	D	C	W	S	U	G	A	R

93

New Testament Books

In the following word hunt see if you can find 25 of the New Testament books. Begin with any letter and move one letter at a time to the right, left, up, down, or diagonally. When you find a word, draw a circle around it.

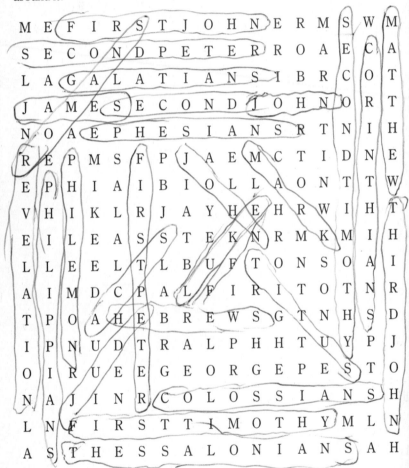

```
M  E  F  I  R  S  T  J  O  H  N  E  R  M  S  W  M
S  E  C  O  N  D  P  E  T  E  R  R  O  A  E  C  A
L  A  G  A  L  A  T  I  A  N  S  I  B  R  C  O  T
J  A  M  E  S  E  C  O  N  D  J  O  H  N  O  R  T
N  O  A  E  P  H  E  S  I  A  N  S  R  T  N  I  H
R  E  P  M  S  F  P  J  A  E  M  C  T  I  D  N  E
E  P  H  I  A  I  B  I  O  L  L  A  O  N  T  T  W
V  H  I  K  L  R  J  A  Y  H  E  H  R  W  I  H  T
E  I  L  E  A  S  S  T  E  K  N  R  M  K  M  I  H
L  L  E  E  L  T  L  B  U  F  T  O  N  S  O  A  I
A  I  M  D  C  P  A  L  F  I  R  I  T  O  T  N  R
T  P  O  A  H  E  B  R  E  W  S  G  T  N  H  S  D
I  P  N  U  D  T  R  A  L  P  H  H  T  U  Y  P  J
O  I  R  U  E  E  G  E  O  R  G  E  P  E  S  T  O
N  A  J  I  N  R  C  O  L  O  S  S  I  A  N  S  H
L  N  F  I  R  S  T  T  I  M  O  T  H  Y  M  L  N
A  S  T  H  E  S  S  A  L  O  N  I  A  N  S  A  H
```

How Many?

1. How many years of warning did God give the people of the world before sending the flood?

   A. 75   B. 100   C. 120   D. 135

2. How many days were Noah and his family in the ark?

   A. 40 days   B. 80 days   C. 225 days   D. 374 days

3. How many times did Abraham plead for Sodom?

   A. 3 times   B. 5 times   C. 6 times   D. 9 times

4. How many years did Jacob serve for both Leah and Rachel?

   A. 5 years   B. 7 years   C. 11 years   D. 14 years

5. How old was Joseph when his brothers sold him into slavery?

   A. 17 years   B. 19 years   C. 21 years   D. 23 years

6. How many years did Jacob live in Egypt?

   A. 15 years   B. 17 years   C. 19 years   D. 21 years

7. How many sisters did Moses' wife have?

   A. 2   B. 4   C. 6   D. 8

8. How many years old was Moses when he stood before Pharaoh?

   A. 70   B. 80   C. 90   D. 100

9. How many years did the Israelites feed on manna?

   A. 20   B. 32   C. 38   D. 40

10. Which year was the year of jubilee?

    A. Every 20th   B. Every 30th   C. Every 40th   D. Every 50th

11. How many cities of refuge were there?

    A. 6   B. 8   C. 10   D. 12

12. How many left-handed soldiers were from the tribe of Benjamin?

    A. 600   B. 700   C. 800   D. 900

Alphagram

Twenty-six words from the Bible are hidden in the diagram on the opposite page. See if you can find them all. There is one word in each row, and one letter is missing from each word. The missing letter may be at the beginning, end, or anyplace within the word. As you fill in the diagram you will find that there are 26 missing letters — one letter for each letter of the alphabet. Since a letter will be used only once, an alphabetical listing has been provided for your assistance. As you use a letter in the diagram, cross it off the alphabetical list.

A B C D E F G H I
J K L M N O P Q R
S T U V W X Y Z

O	N	T	E	M		L	E	N	L	I
R	A	B	D	E		D	M	S	O	H
S	F	E	L	I		C	A	K	P	J
O	H	A	B	A		K	U	K	M	G
G	L	D	I	E		E	A	S	T	K
F	T	A	X	E		B	L	Q	R	F
P	R	S	J	F		I	C	A	H	L
T	K	L	R	O		E	N	J	Y	E
H	Z	E	T	G		U	D	A	S	M
E	A	T	R	A		A	I	L	S	N
I	B	U	F	H		U	E	E	N	D
U	R	E	P	E		T	A	N	C	E
J	D	E	G	B		P	T	I	S	T
D	P	O	T	T		R	Y	P	O	S
K	E	H	F	I		A	R	O	D	S
U	J	A	B	E		K	O	R	O	U
L	G	I	H	J		A	M	E	L	C
M	K	T	P	N		N	E	V	E	H
W	R	C	E	J		H	N	T	A	O
C	T	O	N	G		E	S	S	B	V
D	N	J	U	D		M	E	N	T	E
O	X	A	R	A		A	T	U	I	B
B	E	E	U	T		C	H	U	S	W
P	L	O	B	E		I	E	N	C	E
Q	G	A	L	I		E	E	V	G	S
A	W	F	M	H		O	M	B	A	N

Key Word

To find the key word, fill in the blanks in words 1 through 10 with the correct missing letters. Transfer those letters to the correspondingly numbered squares in the diagram.

1. _B_ L O O D

2. P O O R _E_

3. N _I_ M R O D

4. _D_ E V I L

5. N _E_ B O

6. F I _G_

7. _R_ O B E

8. L I _O_ N

9. C _O_ C K

10. R A N S O _M_

1	2	3	4	5	6	7	8	9	10
B	R	I	D	E	G	R	O	O	m

Hosea's Handkerchief

Help Hosea find his way through the handkerchief maze. You can go only through the white boxes. Go from box to box only if they share a side. No diagonal moves are allowed.

Scripture Alphabets

A   was an emperor who gave a decree. _____

B   was a blind man, anxious to see. _____

C   was a brother who did a great wrong. _____

D   was a teaser who weakened the strong. _____

E   was a twin son, less loved by his mother. _____

F   was a ruler, in place of another. _____

G   was a province, quite frequently named. _____

H   was a tyrant for cruelty famed. _____

I   was a country of mountains and rocks. _____

J   was a shepherd, possessor of flocks. _____

K   was a place where the Ark did repose. _____

L   was a mountain with turban of snows. _____

M   was a priest, as a king also known. _____

N   was a man, whose heart turned as stone. _____

O   was a helper, whose service was kind. _____

P   was a despot of changeable mind. _____

Q   was a queen, as fair as you'll find. _____

R   was a speaker, provokingly rough. _____

S   was a wretch who was punished enough. _____

T   was a disciple, raised from the dead. _____

U   was a land whence came Israel's head. _____

V   was a wife who refused so to be. _____

W   was an animal, found in the sea. _____

Y   was for Timothy, and so let it be. _____

Z   was for a short man who climbed a tree. _____

Birds of the Bible

In the following word hunt see if you can find 31 birds of the Bible. Begin with any letter and move one letter at a time to the right, left, up, or down. When you find a word, draw a circle around it.

```
L  K  I  T  E  P  E  A  C  O  C  K  G  J  H  T  O
H  E  A  V  L  N  Y  T  Q  U  A  I  L  H  O  O  S
C  O  C  K  S  W  A  L  L  O  W  H  E  R  O  N  T
C  D  O  V  E  S  W  A  L  B  L  O  D  O  P  P  R
O  M  R  O  B  I  M  C  H  I  C  K  E  N  O  A  I
W  L  M  T  O  N  I  G  H  T  H  A  W  K  E  R  C
B  H  O  E  A  G  J  L  P  T  A  O  W  J  E  R  H
L  C  R  V  U  L  T  U  R  E  W  S  T  O  R  K  S
C  R  A  N  E  C  H  A  W  R  R  A  V  E  T  Y  P
H  O  N  J  P  U  P  E  L  N  B  L  U  E  B  I  A
A  V  T  S  I  C  S  E  L  L  A  P  W  I  N  G  R
W  E  A  G  G  K  F  A  L  C  O  N  D  O  V  R  R
K  B  H  O  E  O  H  G  B  A  O  S  P  R  E  Y  O
H  I  P  P  O  W  E  L  B  I  R  D  B  A  R  D  W
S  W  A  N  N  G  R  E  A  T  O  W  L  V  U  C  A
K  R  P  E  L  I  C  A  N  R  W  O  R  E  E  A  L
L  P  A  R  T  R  I  D  G  E  L  F  L  N  M  I  N
```

Alphabet Fill-in

The 26 letters of the alphabet are missing from the puzzle below. See if you can place them where they belong. You can cross the letters off as you use them.

A B C D E F G H I J K L M
N O P Q R S T U V W X Y Z

Answers

Answers

Page 7

Who Said It?

1. David — Psalm 23:1
2. Jeremiah — Jeremiah 17:5
3. David — Psalm 103:12
4. Jeremiah — Jeremiah 6:14
5. Solomon — Proverbs 13:15
6. Solomon — Ecclesiastes 12:12
7. Solomon — Proverbs 15:1
8. Agur — Proverbs 30:8
9. Solomon — Proverbs 19:14
10. Solomon — Proverbs 23:2

Page 8

Quotation Puzzle

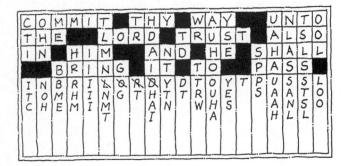

Psalm 37:5

Answers

Help Lydia

Answers

Occupation Match

1. G
2. F
3. H
4. O
5. J
6. D
7. A
8. L
9. E
10. N
11. M
12. C
13. K
14. I
15. B

Answers

Things That
Happen With
Conversion

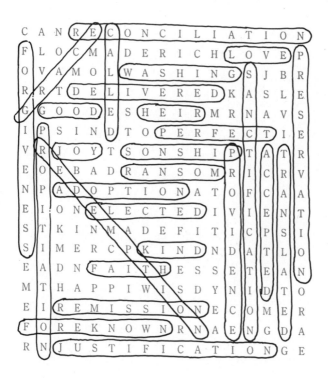

Answers

Page 12

Jacob

1. G
2. H
3. E
4. K
5. C
6. A
7. D, L
8. L
9. F, L
10. L, I, A
11. A, B, J
12. M

Page 14

Bible Labyrinth

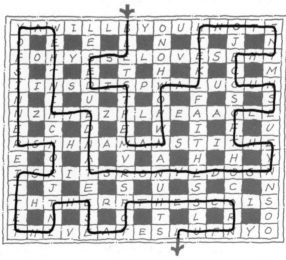

Psalm 1:1

Answers

Page 15

Name the Event

"For she said within herself, 'If I but touch his garment, I shall be whole.' "

Matthew 9:21

Page 16

Versigram

1. Come unto me, all ye that labour and are heavy laden, and I will give you rest — Matthew 11:28.
2. For the Son of man is come to seek and to save that which was lost — Luke 19:10.
3. There shall not any man be able to stand before thee all the days of thy life: as I was with Moses, so I will be with thee: I will not fail thee, nor forsake thee — Joshua 1:5.
4. Jesus answered and said unto him, "Verily, verily I say unto thee, except a man be born again, he cannot see the kingdom of God" — John 3:3.
5. And God called the firmament Heaven. And the evening and the morning were the second day — Genesis 1:8.

Answers

Page 17

Quotation Puzzle

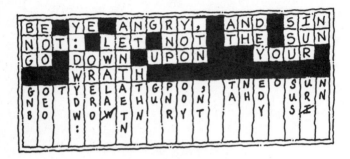

Ephesians 4:26

Answers

A Special Name

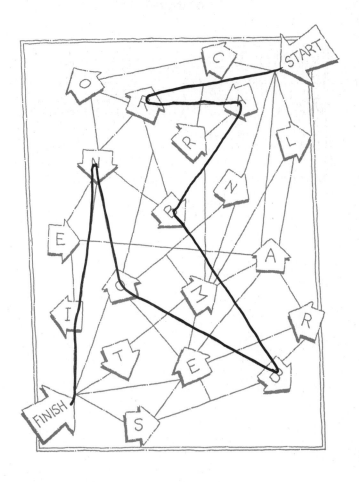

Answers

How Long?

1. C — Exodus 2:2
2. B — Exodus 24:16
3. A — Leviticus 23:34
4. B — Numbers 13:25
5. C — Numbers 19:11
6. C — Deuteronomy 24:5

7. B — 2 Samuel 2:11
8. A — 1 Kings 6:38
9. B — Job 3:13
10. A — 2 Chronicles 36:20,21
11. B — Jonah 3:4
12. C — Exodus 7:25

Page 20

Paul's Puzzle

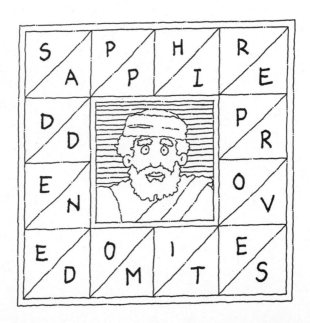

Answers

A Very Famous Place

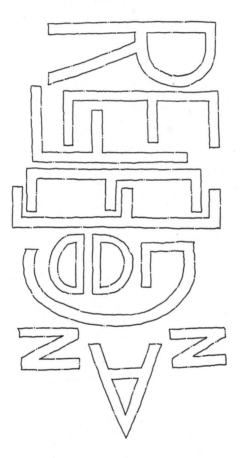

Answer: Garden of Eden

Answers

Page 22, 23

Isaac
Genesis 24:1 – 35:29

1. B. — His kindred
2. Under Abraham's thigh
3. D. — Rebekah
4. Bethuel
5. A. — Keturah
6. False. He was 175 years old.
7. Jacob and Esau
8. Esau
9. Jacob, C. — heel
10. Red
11. Esau
12. False. It was the younger son who stole the blessing.
13. A. — 180

Page 24

Name the Event

The wedding at Cana
"Jesus said to the servants, 'Fill the jars with water.' "

John 2:7 (NIV)

Answers

Forgiveness —
70 x 7

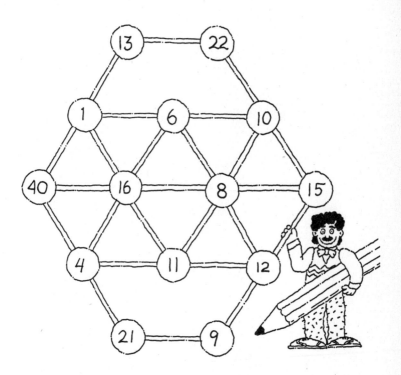

Answers

Humorous Bible
Riddles

1. He broke all of the commandments at once
2. In the beginning (big-inning)
3. Samson — he brought the house down
4. Adam — he was first in the human race
5. Because it was without an Eve
6. Joshua — he was the son of Nun
7. When he went to Philippi (Phil-i-ppi)
8. Because they are generally the same people
9. When God drove Adam and Eve out of the Garden
10. Adam 8-1-2

Page 27

Kings for the
Scholar

1. A — 1 Kings 14:20
2. C — 1 Kings 15:25
3. G — 1 Kings 15:33
4. C — 1 Kings 16:8
5. J — 1 Kings 16:15
6. E — 1 Kings 16:23
7. A — 1 Kings 16:29
8. C — 1 Kings 22:51
9. E — 2 Kings 3:1
10. H — 2 Kings 10:36
11. B — 2 Kings 13:1
12. I — 2 Kings 13:10
13. D — 2 Kings 14:23
14. L — 2 Kings 15:8
15. K — 2 Kings 15:13
16. F — 2 Kings 15:17
17. C — 2 Kings 15:23
18. N — 2 Kings 15:27
19. M — 2 Kings 17:1

Answers

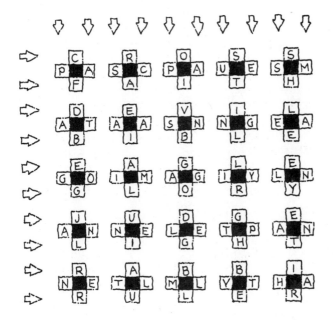

Priscilla's
Problem

Answers

Jumbles

SCRAMBLED NAME	UNSCRAMBLED NAME
1. HSEPJO	J (O) S E P (H)
HLIATGO	G O (L) (I) A T H
PMEHRIA	E (P) H R A I (M)
NEAR	(E) R A (N)

New scrambled name (O) (H) (L) (I) (P) (M) (E) (N)
Unscrambled name PHILEMON

2. EEEEBDZ	(Z) E B E D E E
NEBUER	(R) E (U) B E N
UASL	(S) A U (L)
ACAANN	C A N (A) (A) N

New scrambled name (Z) (R) (U) (S) (L) (A) (A)
Unscrambled name LAZARUS

Answers

Page 30

The Ten
Commandments

Thou shalt have no other gods before me.
Thou shalt not make unto thee any graven image.
Thou shalt not take the name of the Lord thy God in vain.
Remember the sabbath day to keep it holy.
Honor thy father and mother.
Thou shalt not kill.
Thou shalt not commit adultery.
Thou shalt not steal.
Thou shalt not bear false witness against thy neighbor.
Thou shalt not covet thy neighbor's house . . . nor any thing that is thy
neighbor's.

Exodus 20:3-17

Answers

Bible Occupations

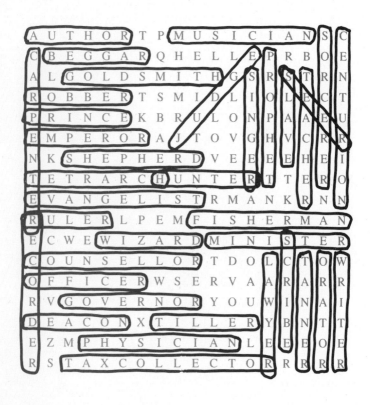

Answers

Page 32

The Good Samaritan

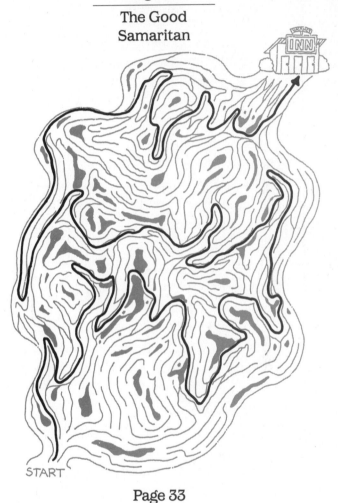

START

Page 33

Name the Event

"And Absalom rode upon a mule, and the mule went under the thick boughs of a great oak, and his head caught hold of the oak . . . and the mule that was under him went away."

2 Samuel 18:9

Answers

Page 34

Tail Tag

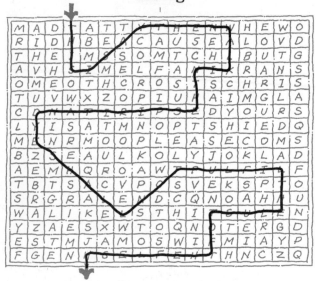

Galatians 5:16

Page 35

Vocation Match

1. J — Judges 4:1-16
2. K — Acts 24:1
3. L — 1 Chronicles 15:19
4. M — Matthew 27:16
5. N — Acts 16:14
6. O — 2 Kings 4:12
7. B — Genesis 4:2
8. A — Genesis 4:22

9. C — Philemon 10-16
10. D — Acts 8:9
11. E — Titus 3:13
12. F — Acts 18:2,3
13. G — 2 Timothy 4:14
14. H — 2 Timothy 2:17,18
15. I — Acts 10:6

Answers

Page 36

Name the Event

"He had compassion on him, and went to him, and bound up his wounds, pouring in oil and wine."

Luke 10:34

Answers

A Special Place

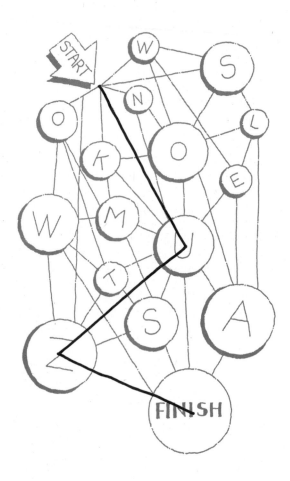

Answers

Page 38

Guess Who

1. Eglon — Judges 3:16-25
2. Jesus and Peter — Matthew 14:25-29
3. Matthew — Matthew 9:9 and Luke 5:27
4. Simon — Matthew 4:18
5. Peter, James, John, Moses, and Elijah — Mark 9:2-4
6. Pilate — John 19:15,16
7. Martha — Luke 10:40
8. Lazarus — Luke 16:23
9. Zacchaeus — Luke 19:2
10. Lazarus — John 11:1,2
11. Nicodemus — John 3:1,2
12. Theophilus — Acts 1:1
13. Matthias — Acts 1:25,26
14. Ananias and Sapphira — Acts 5:1-10
15. Gamaliel — Acts 5:34-39
16. Stephen — Acts 7:59,60
17. Philip — Acts 8:26-35
18. Cornelius — Acts 10:1-48
19. Tertius — Romans 16:22
20. Philemon — Philemon 1-16

Page 39

Patchword

1. Zealot
2. Nicodemus
3. Corinthians
4. Synagogue
5. Gamaliel
6. Nicolaitans
7. Tiberius
8. Eutychus
9. Predestination
10. Lamentations

Answers

Page 40, 41

The Sons
of Jacob

1. Dan — Bilhah
2. Levi — Leah
3. Gad — Zilpah
4. Benjamin — Rachel
5. Reuben — Leah
6. Zebulun — Leah
7. Naphtali — Bilhah
8. Simeon — Leah
9. Asher — Zilpah
10. Judah — Leah
11. Issachar — Leah
12. Joseph — Rachel
13. In the hollow of his thigh — Genesis 32:25
14. Israel — Genesis 32:28
15. Peniel — Genesis 32:30
16. God, face, face — Genesis 32:30
17. 400 — Genesis 33:1
18. B. Dinah — Genesis 30:21
19. Benjamin — Genesis 35:16-19

Page 42

Patchword

1. Sanballat
2. Sacrifice
3. Sapphira
4. Tyrannus
5. Pamphylia
6. Pharaoh
10. Rebekah
7. Perfume
8. Damascus
9. Samaritans

Answers

Page 43

Hannah's Headache

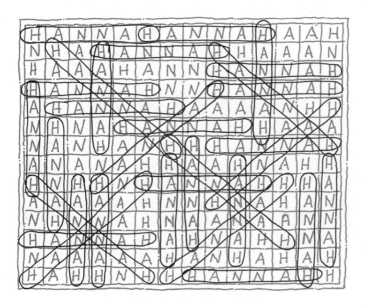

Answers

Page 44

Peter's Path

But grow in grace and in the knowledge of our Lord and Savior Jesus Christ. To him be glory both now and for ever. Amen.

Page 45

Quotation Puzzle

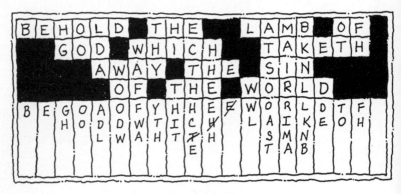

John 1:29

Answers

Page 46

Bible Labyrinth

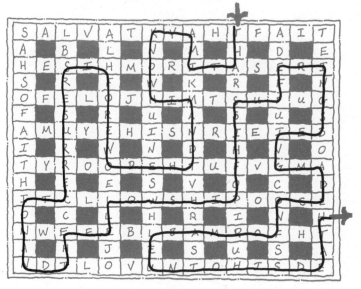

Philippians 3:10

Page 47

Names and Meanings Match

1. J   9. M
2. D   10. A
3. G   11. L
4. F   12. N
5. H   13. K
6. O   14. E
7. B   15. I
8. C

Answers

Quotation Puzzle

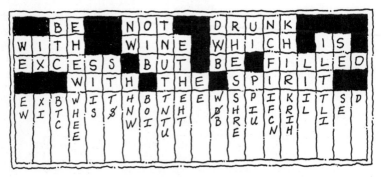

Ephesians 5:18

Answers

Page 49

Key Word

1. Alpha
2. Nile
3. Paran
4. Child
5. Bed
6. Amen
7. Magi
8. King
9. Poet
10. Brass

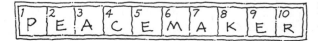

Page 50

Alphabet Fill-in

Answers

Page 51

Son Rays

Page 52

Who Said It?

1. Jeremiah — Jeremiah 17:9
2. John — Revelation 7:17
3. God — Hosea 4:17
4. John — 1 John 4:18
5. God — Amos 3:3
6. Peter — 1 Peter 4:8 (NIV)
7. Jesus — Matthew 6:29
8. James — James 2:18
9. Paul — 1 Thessalonians 5:21
10. Paul — 1 Timothy 6:6

Answers

Page 53

Pharaoh's Diamond

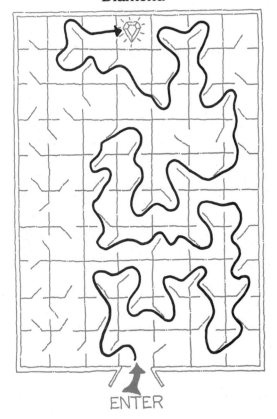

ENTER

Answers

Page 54

Bible Anagram

1. Ner — 1 Samuel 14:50
2. Ezra — Ezra 7:11
3. Bezer — Deuteronomy 4:43
4. Uz — Job 1:1
5. Cana — John 2:1
6. Hur — Exodus 17:12
7. Abana — 2 Kings 5:12
8. Dan — Genesis 49:16
9. Nun — Numbers 27:18,19
10. Ehud — Judges 3:15
11. Zeeb — Judges 7:25
12. Zebah — Judges 8:5
13. Abner — 2 Samuel 2:8
14. Reuben — Genesis 49:1-3

The King's name is Nebuchadnezzar — Daniel 3:1-23

Page 55

Quotation Puzzle

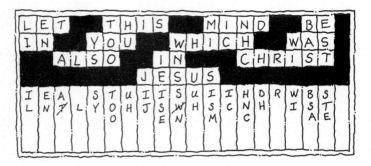

Philippians 2:5

Answers

Jumbles

SCRAMBLED NAME	UNSCRAMBLED NAME
1. V D I A D	(D) A V (I) D
B J O	J (O) (B)
A D N	D (A) N
A A H M N	(H) A M (A) N

New scrambled name (D) (I) (O) (B) (A) (H) (A)
Unscrambled name   O B A D I A H

2. A P E P A R H S	(E) P A P H (R) A (S)
B C E A L	(C) A (L) E B
E D G I O N	G (I) D E (O) N
A N H U M	(N) A H (U) M

New scrambled name   (E) (R) (S) (C) (L) (I) (O) (N) (U)
Unscrambled name   C O R N E L I U S

Quotation Puzzle

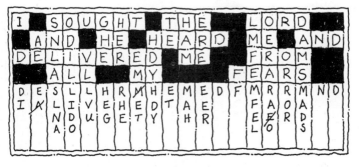

Psalm 34:4

Answers

Page 58, 59

Syl-La-Puzzle

1. Hypocrite
2. Disciple
3. Ointment
4. Tabernacle
5. Conversion
6. Devotions
7. Repent
8. Worship
9. Evangelist
10. Nicodemus
11. Nathanael
12. Obadiah
13. Lazarus
14. Timothy
15. Redeemer
16. Melchizedek
17. Nehemiah
18. Bartimaeus
19. Salvation
20. Nazareth

Page 60

Tail Tag

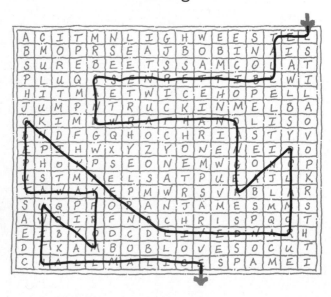

Ephesians 4:31

Answers

Page 61

Choose-A-Letter

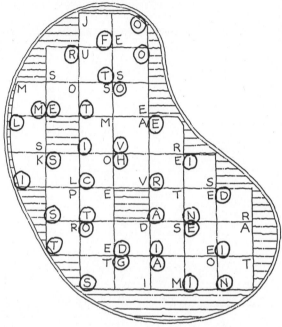

"For to me to live is Christ, and to die is gain" (Philippians 1:21).

Page 62

Quotation Puzzle

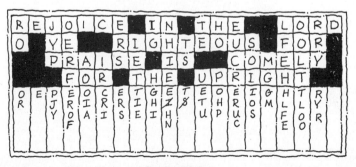

Psalm 33:1

137

Answers

Name the Event

"How many hired servants of my father's have bread enough and to spare, and I perish with hunger!"

Luke 15:17

Page 64, 65

Alphagram

		O	A	T	H					
P	A	T	R	I	A	R	C	H		
				E	X	I	L	E		
	M	A	R	A	N	A	T	H	A	
					Q	U	A	I	L	S
		P	R	O	V	E	R	B	S	
		C	O	R	I	N	T	H		
P	R	A	Y	E	R					
				N	U	M	B	E	R	S
		L	A	Z	A	R	U	S		
	L	A	M	B						
		O	M	E	G	A				
	S	A	M	S	O	N				
				L	O	G	O	S		
	M	O	R	D	E	C	A	I		
		M	U	S	I	C				
		M	A	G	I					
		L	A	W						
	P	Y	R	A	M	I	D	S		
		E	G	Y	P	T				
				P	H	I	L	I	P	
	L	E	V	I	T	E	S			
				C	R	O	S	S		
				K	A	D	E	S	H	
				F	L	O	O	D		
				J	U	D	G	E	S	

Answers

Page 66

Patchword

1. Galatians
2. Obadiah
3. Zechariah
4. Frankincense
5. Affliction
6. Believers
7. Gnosticism
8. Regeneration
9. Nehemiah
10. Leaven
11. Communion
12. Conscience
13. Covenant
14. Lucifer
15. Justification

Page 67

Jumbles

SCRAMBLED NAME
1. WTTHMAE
   FXILE
   HUDE
   SAMDE

UNSCRAMBLED NAME
M (A) (T) T (H) (E) W
F (E) (L) I X
E (H) (U) D
D E (M) A (S)

New scrambled name (A) (T) (H) (E) (E) (L) (H) (U) (M) (S)
Unscrambled name METHUSELAH

2. SITUT
   DHREO
   OANH
   ETRPE

(T) I T U (S)
H (E) R O D
(N) O A (H)
(P) E T (E) R

New scrambled name (T) (S) (E) (N) (H) (P) (E)
Unscrambled name STEPHEN

Answers

Page 68

Find
the Angel

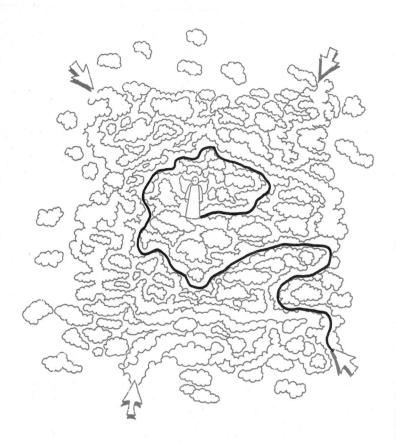

Answers

Page 69

Who Said It?

1. Joseph — Genesis 37:16
2. Elijah — 1 Kings 17:1
3. Joseph — Genesis 40:19
4. Moses — Exodus 4:1
5. Elijah — 1 Kings 19:4
6. Moses — Exodus 33:18
7. Elijah — 1 Kings 18:30
8. Joseph — Genesis 39:9
9. Moses — Deuteronomy 32:11
10. Elijah — 1 Kings 18:44
11. Joseph — Genesis 41:33
12. Elijah — 1 Kings 18:21
13. Moses — Exodus 20:20
14. Joseph — Genesis 50:19
15. Moses — Exodus 14:13

Page 70

Alphabet Fill-in

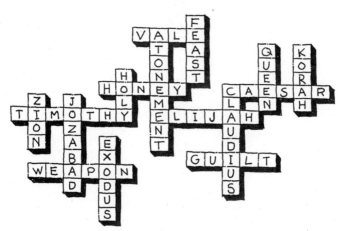

Answers

Page 71

Something
Noah Found

Noah found grace in the eyes of the Lord — Genesis 6:8.

Page 72

Key Word

1. Agape
2. Age
3. Gentile
4. Stephen
5. Achan
6. Prophet
7. Daniel
8. Uncle
9. Scorpion
10. Ahab

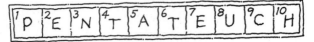

Page 73

Name the Event

"Bear ye one another's burdens."

Galatians 6:2

Answers

Page 74

Bishops and Deacons

1. Blameless
2. Husband of one wife
3. Vigilant
4. Sober
5. Good behavior
6. Given to hospitality
7. Apt to teach
8. Not given to wine
9. Not a striker (not quarrelsome)
10. Not greedy for money
11. Patient
12. Not a brawler
13. Not covetous
14. Obedient children
15. Not a new Christian
16. A good reputation
17. Not doubletongued
18. Pure conscience

Page 75

Old Testament Characters

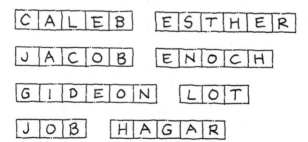

CALEB   ESTHER

JACOB   ENOCH

GIDEON   LOT

JOB   HAGAR

Answers

Who Said It?

1. God — Genesis 8:21
2. Abraham — Genesis 18:25
3. Moses — Deuteronomy 19:21
4. God — Leviticus 19:18
5. Balaam — Numbers 23:10
6. Moses — Numbers 32:23
7. God — Zechariah 2:8
8. Samuel — 1 Samuel 13:14
9. Queen of Sheba — 1 Kings 10:7
10. Job — Job 5:7

A Place for Everyone

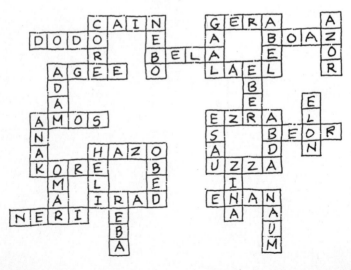

Answers

Page 78

Famous Prisoners

1. Joseph
2. Samson
3. Jeremiah
4. Daniel
5. John the Baptist
6. Jesus
7. Peter

8. Paul
9. Silas
10. Shadrach
11. Meshach
12. Abednego
13. Joseph
14. Barabbas

Page 79

Bible Labyrinth

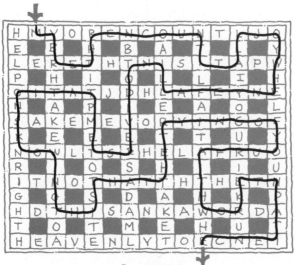

James 1:2,3

Answers

Page 80

Guess Who

1. Micah — Micah 5:2
2. Malachi — Malachi 1:1 – 4:6
3. Samson — Judges 16:3
4. Ruth — Ruth 1:16
5. Eli — 1 Samuel 3:12,13
6. Delilah — Judges 16:18, 19
7. Boaz — Ruth 4:9, 10
8. Saul — 1 Samuel 10:24
9. Samuel — 1 Samuel 15:16-26
10. Jonathan — 1 Samuel 18:1
11. Michal — 1 Samuel 18:27
12. Mephibosheth — 2 Samuel 9:3-6
13. Uriah — 2 Samuel 11:14-17
14. Absalom — 2 Samuel 18:9
15. Elijah — 1 Kings 17:1-4
16. Ahab — 1 Kings 21:1, 2
17. Jezebel — 2 Kings 9:35-37
18. Enoch — Genesis 5:24
19. Naaman — 2 Kings 5:9-14
20. Solomon — 1 Kings 7:51

Page 81

Who Wrote Romans?

Answers

Versigram

1. The Lord also will be a refuge for the oppressed, a refuge in times of trouble — Psalm 9:9.
2. For even the Son of man came not to be ministered unto, but to minister, and to give his life a ransom for many — Mark 10:45.
3. The heart is deceitful above all things, and desperately wicked; who can know it? — Jeremiah 17:9.
4. And it shall come to pass, that whosoever shall call on the name of the Lord shall be saved — Acts 2:21.
5. To an inheritance incorruptible, and undefiled, and that fadeth not away, reserved in heaven for you — 1 Peter 1:4.

Page 83

Mixed Letters

Nathanael — John 1:46

Page 84

Jumbles

SCRAMBLED NAME	UNSCRAMBLED NAME
1. R A N A O	A (A) R O N
N A A C H	A C (H) A N
W R E N A D	A N D (R) (E) W
B G A U S A	A G A B U (S)

New scrambled name   (A) (H) (R) (E) (S)
Unscrambled name   A S H E R

2. X X T A R R A E E S	A R T A (X) (E) (R) X E S
M A L A E K	(A) M A (L) (E) K
M D A A	A (D) A M
K N A A	(A) (N) A K

New scrambled name   (X) (E) (R) (A) (L) (E) (D) (A) (N)
Unscrambled name   A L E X A N D E R

Answers

Page 85

Alphanumber

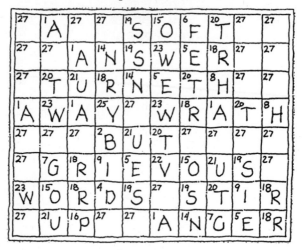

Proverbs 15:1

Page 86

Key Word

1. Altar
2. Ammon
3. Abel
4. Enosh
5. Aaron
6. Dathan
7. Law
8. Cherub
9. Felix
10. Bread

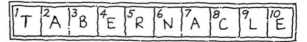

Answers

Page 87

Humorous
Bible Riddles

1. Down in the mouth
2. When he slept with his forefathers
3. They raised Cain
4. On the side of his head
5. Who else?
6. To avoid Egyptian traffic
7. Job — he had the most patience (patients)
8. Joseph — Pharaoh made a ruler out of him
9. When Joseph served in Pharaoh's court
10. When the evil spirits entered into the pigs

Page 88

Patchword

1. Ishmael
2. Demetrius
3. Syntyche
4. Apocalypse
5. Ascension
6. Beersheba
10. Praetorium
7. Laodicea
8. Mephibosheth
9. Onesimus

Answers

Page 89

Quotation Puzzle

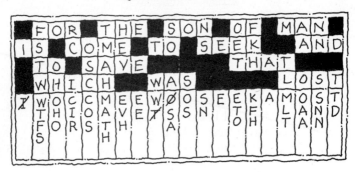

Page 90

Bartimeus' Bubbles

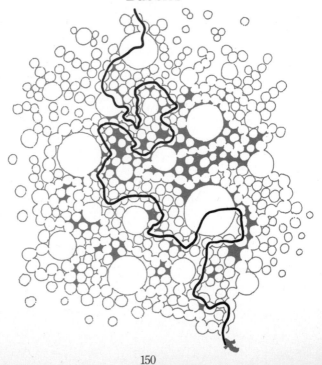

Answers

Page 91

Lipogram

1. For with God nothing shall be impossible — Luke 1:37.
2. In the beginning God created the heaven and the earth — Genesis 1:1.
3. As newborn babes, desire the sincere milk of the word, that ye may grow thereby — 1 Peter 2:2.
4. For I am not ashamed of the gospel of Christ: for it is the power of God unto salvation to every one that believeth; to the Jew first, and also to the Greek — Romans 1:16.
5. Blessed is the man that walketh not in the counsel of the ungodly, nor standeth in the way of sinners, nor sitteth in the seat of the scornful. But his delight is in the law of the Lord; and in his law doth he meditate day and night — Psalm 1:1,2.

Page 92

Name the Event

Parable of the ten virgins

Matthew 25:1-13

Answers

Page 93

Tail Tag

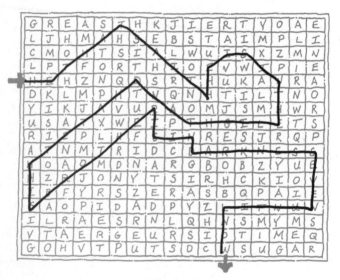

1 John 2:9

Answers

Page 94

New Testament Books

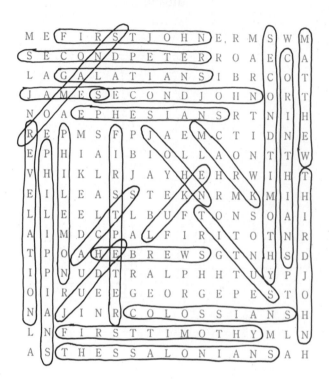

Page 95

How Many?

1. C — Genesis 6:3
2. D — Genesis 7:10, 11; 8:14-16
3. C — Genesis 18:23-32
4. D — Genesis 29:20-30
5. A — Genesis 37:2
6. B — Genesis 47:28
7. C — Genesis 2:16
8. B — Exodus 7:7
9. D — Exodus 16:35
10. D — Leviticus 25:11
11. A — Numbers 35:13
12. B — Judges 20:15,16

Answers

Page 96, 97

Alphagram

		T	E	M	P	L	E			
			D	E	W					
	F	E	L	I	X					
	H	A	B	A	K	K	U	K		
				F	E	A	S	T		
	T	A	X	E	S					
				M	I	C	A	H		
		R	O	B	E					
				J	U	D	A	S		
	T	R	A	V	A	I	L			
				Q	U	E	E	N		
	R	E	P	E	N	T	A	N	C	E
				B	A	P	T	I	S	T
	P	O	T	T	E	R	Y			
				H	A	R	O	D		
	J	A	B	E	Z					
				C	A	M	E	L		
			N	I	N	E	V	E	H	
			J	O	H	N				
	T	O	N	G	U	E	S			
		J	U	D	G	M	E	N	T	
		A	R	A	R	A	T			
		E	U	T	Y	C	H	U	S	
		O	B	E	D	I	E	N	C	E
	G	A	L	I	L	E	E			
				T	O	M	B			

Page 98

Key Word

1. Blood 3. Nimrod 5. Nebo 7. Robe 9. Cock
2. Poor   4. Devil   6. Fig   8. Lion 10. Ransom

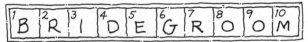

¹B	²R	³I	⁴D	⁵E	⁶G	⁷R	⁸O	⁹O	¹⁰M

Answers

Page 99

Hosea's
Handkerchief

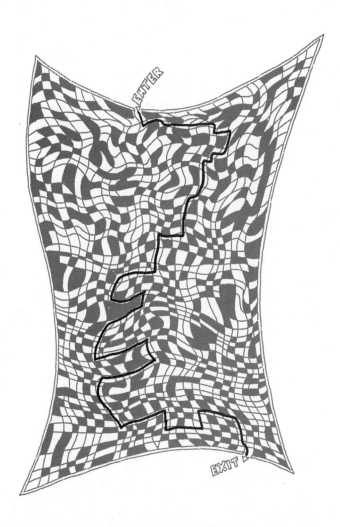

Answers

Scripture
Alphabets

A — ugustus — Luke 2:1
B — artimaeus — Mark 10:46,52
C — ain — Genesis 4:8
D — elilah — Judges 16:4,15-21
E — sau — Genesis 25:24-28
F — estus — Acts 24:27
G — alilee — Matthew 3:13
H — erod — Matthew 2:16
I — dumea — Isaiah 34:5
J — acob — Genesis 32:7
K — irjathjearim — 1 Samuel 7:2
L — ebanon — Jeremiah 18:14
M — elchizedek — Genesis 14:18
N — abal — 1 Samuel 25:37
O — nesiphorus — 2 Timothy 1:16,18
P — haraoh — Exodus 8:28,32
Q — ueen Esther — Esther 2:15
R — abshakeh — 2 Kings 18:19,25
S — ennacherib — 2 Kings 19:35-37
T — abitha — Acts 9:36,41
U — r — Nehemiah 9:7
V — ashti — Esther 1:12
W — hale — Genesis 1:21
Y — outhful — 1 Timothy 4:12
Z — acchaeus — Luke 19:2-4

Answers

Page 101

Birds of the Bible

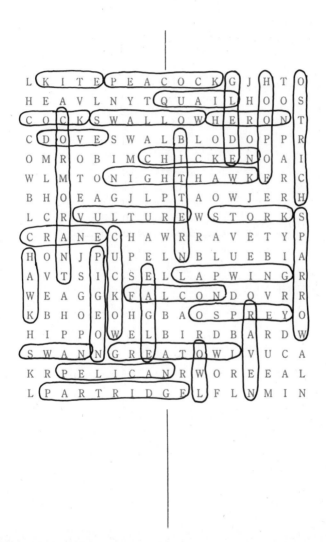

Answers

Alphabet Fill-in

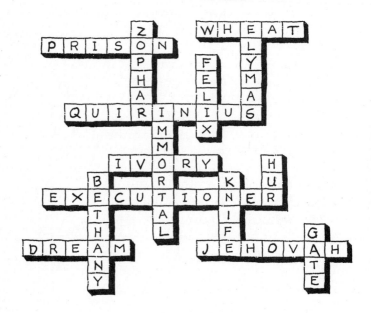

Other Books by Bob Phillips

For information on how to purchase any of the above books, contact your local bookstore or send a self-addressed stamped envelope to:

Family Services
P.O. Box 9363
Fresno, CA 93702

Books by Vern McClellan

WISE WORDS FROM A WISE GUY

Back with his latest collection of the wise and wacky,
master wordsmith Vern McLellan is ready to brighten
your life and conversation with illustrated principles
and humor based on the sayings of Solomon and others.

SHREDDED WIT

A "bran" new serving of insightful bitefuls of wit and
wisdom. Supplement your diet with hundreds of
delightful and inspirational morsels of high-fiber humor.

PROVERBS FOR PEOPLE

Clever proverbs are matched with a corresponding
Scripture reference and illustration that will bring a smile
and a cause for reflection with the turn of each page.

QUIPS, QUOTES, AND QUESTS

You will never be without a wise or witty saying after
you read *Quips, Quotes, and Quests*. This compilation
of famous (and infamous) Bible verses, quotations, and
sayings is a handy reference for the whole family.

PROVERBS, PROMISES, AND PRINCIPLES

A stimulating new collection of thought-provoking sayings
and colorful anecdotes to give your life and conversation
a lift. Contains hundreds of new topics handled in a
skillful and readable style.